HOW TO BECOME A FAMOUS ARTIST THROUGH PAIN AND SUFFERING

PLUS other almost true-to-life essays uncovering the hitherto rarely before-revealed secrets of the art world...shhh.

Simon Press   Portland, Oregon

1

©1996 by Arne Westerman

Published by Simon Press, 711 SW Alder #313
Portland Oregon 97205

Library of Congress Catalog Card Number: 95-071221

ISBN Number: 0-9649538-1-1

10 9 8 7 6 5 4 3 2 1

Cover Design and Cartoons by Frank Farah
(He is the best according to an independent survey.)

Cover Photo by Ancil Nance
No slouch either!

Dedication

Dedicated with much love to my Sis, Gladys, who has always been supportive of me and who shares all our history.

And to the little ones, some of whom aren't so little any more. To Lauren and Daniel Gehman; Hannah and Max Westerman; Emily, Carrie, Katie, Ellen and Clair Charlton; and all the little ones who haven't made their formal appearances yet.

Acknowledgments

Special thanks to my wife, Judy Westerman, who sparked a lot of great ideas and helped edit. I am especially indebted to my editor, Rachel Wolf, for her thoughtful suggestions and consummate expertise.

To Margie Boulé for her thoughts on sharpening and rearranging material. To Judy Gehman for thorough copyediting. If you find any words misspelled, blame her or Windows 95.

To Dr. Herb Freeman, Bruce Dodson, Daniel Goldberg, Cheap Joe Miller, Burt Silverman, Marty Westerman and Milt Kobayashi for their ideas and support.

If I ever have this book put on tape, I'll ask Pearl and Bernard Galitzki to do the reading. They do it with such flair.

To my non-existent research team for not interfering in my madness and to all those who only stand and serve.

My sincere thanks.

Introduction
by Burt Silverman

What a delight to finally read a book about art that is fun and sensible and witty and shreds the pretentiousness of so much contemporary critical writing.

The very title How to Become A Famous Artist Through Pain And Suffering *touches on the fundamental speciousness of the conventional notion of genius. And indeed it suggests that art need not deal solely with life's agonies in order to be meaningful.*

Throughout this warmly good natured book – and it is funny! -- there is a serious understanding of the everyday problems of creating art and of trying to get it seen by other than family and friends.

Chapters such as the Origin of the Paintbrush *and* Ask the Art Expert *– are marvelous satires on art history as indeed are others that puncture our art culture's obsessive need for novelty like* Niche-ing, *and* Sandscor Dingbat, Underwater Painter, *and culminate in the* New Interactive Videotape Demonstration.

Arne Westerman is genuinely inventive and creative as a painter. He is equally at home with words. Take a few hours out of the quotidian anxiety of making pictures and relax with this wonderfully engaging and yes! -- thought provoking, book.

Apology

Other instructional Pain and Suffering Books scheduled for release in time for major events:

- **How To Become A World-Famous Plumber** *Through Pain And Suffering*
- **How To Train Your Parakeet To Sell Insurance Over The Phone**
- **How To Become Famous For 15 Minutes** *Through Pain And Suffering*
- **How To Turn Yourself Into A Frog And Attract Passing Princesses or How To Turn Yourself Into a Princess and Attract Frogs**
- **How To Teach Your Cat To Scarf Down Sale-Priced Cat Food**
- **How To Hypnotize Your Computer And Force Your Will Upon It** *Through Pain And Suffering*
- **How To Tell Funny Banana Stories In Public** *Through Pain And Suffering*
- **How To Attract Strangers With Card Tricks** Through Pain And Suffering
- **How To Legally Change Your Birth Sign**
- *AND OTHER WORLD TOPICS*

Books by Arne Westerman

Paint Watercolors Filled With Life and Energy
By Arne Westerman
North Light Books Cincinnatti OH

- Books featuring Westerman Paintings by North Light Books, Cincinnati OH:

Splash 1
Splash 4
Being an Artist
Artist's Guide to Materials and Techniques

- From Rockport Publishers, Rockport MA

The Best of Watercolors

Contents

"What a splendid way to express my
agony," thought Goya.

Chapter 1

How To Become A Famous Artist Through Pain And Suffering

Anyone who has ever seen

a movie about an artist knows that at one time or another the central character will undergo great suffering. Almost as much as the audience.

Name any painter, sculptor, opera star, ballet dancer, instrumentalist, composer, or whoever in the movie, and he or she will go through tears of agony before becoming a star.

Even a dummy knows that. Somewhere in the picture the audience will be inundated with crying and shrying and moaning and groaning and sickness and dying and movie actors will be artfully dodging flying bits of ears.

Artists portrayed in movies never hit pay dirt without living through the Hell of hunger, fear, unrequited love, jealousy, rage, and madness. Not to mention poor diet or lousy leftovers, unfair critical reviews, the public's ignorance or bad taste or lack of understanding.

Suffering In Art Class Not Considered Turning Point

Sure, a painter may suffer through an art class on perspective or drawing trees or reading *Art News*, but that's not the kind of misery that marks a crisis or the big turning point in a film. Not usually.

So take a page from Hollywood and remember that our work, like that of any artist, improves with misery. Sorry, but that's what it takes.

Why else are the works of painters called "paintings," or *pain - tings,* which is derived from the ancient Celtic phrase, *"PAYN THUINGS,"* meaning *"pained picture maker who suffers regularly from the curse of heartburn."*

Some Tormented Examples

The first cave paintings were created by a headstrong woman artist named Muffie. Women had to be particularly headstrong in those bygone days since love and affection were regularly expressed by clubs to their craniums.

Archaeologists now tell us that the Lascaux cave paintings evolved from this specific type of suffering. Thus we learn that Muffie, the first Pre-Magnet artist, threw in the towel and said, "to heck with it!" She then retired to the Lascaux cave in France, painted animals from memory and became the world's first practicing vegetarian.

Ever since, pain and suffering have been handmaidens to the creation of quality art. Every artist of consequence has endured it -- even welcomed it. Masterpieces don't just pop out of folks who are happy as clams.

For instance, suffering was no novelty to Leonardo who worked on the Mona Lisa for five years and finally gave up on her smile and took up drinking and designing airplanes.

Rubens had his share of pain, too, but he used a process called *transference*. In his painting, *Rape of the Daughters of Lecippus,* he transferred his own personal agony to the faces of two of his soldier models. Following their posing sessions carrying around those overweight "daughters," they were both hospitalized for hemorrhoids, altoids and herniated discs.

Talk about pain! Francisco Jose Goya had more than his share of suffering in the court of Carlos IV in Spain, painting portraits of some of the ugliest people on earth.

Van Gogh suffered TOO heavily throughout his career but never really profited from the experience. He didn't know when to quit.

That's why one of his paintings recently sold for forty million bucks and he didn't get a cent. Take that as a piece of good advice! Torment and torture are all well and good for improving one's art, but you must agonize wisely and never overdo.

Any artist can learn to suffer. The main trick is to make it show up in your work. You've already had a good start with those rejections from juried shows, galleries, a cheap and fickle public and critics who ignore you.

Combine that with your own less-than-pleased opinion of many of your paintings plus your smoldering envy of other artists and you are halfway to your goal already!

Should You Be On Maintenance?

Before starting any daily program of fruitful agony, it's important you find out if you already have enough to produce masterpieces or whether you need additional miseries.

That's why we recommend you take the following quiz to get a fix on your personal pain quotient.

Take This Test Now

1. Do you think your work is unappreciated and you are misunderstood?
2. Did you ever have the misfortune to study art with _____ ? (Name of teacher.)
3. Is your child the one with the body piercings and green porcupine hair who asked me for spare change yesterday?
4. Are you presently living with (name)_____or did you ever suffer that fate?
5. Do you always feel guilty but can't remember why?
6. Are you still sorry?
7. Is your neighbor the one with the big dog who knows exactly when you're going to mow your lawn?
8. Do you cry at movies even when it just reads, "No Smoking" on the screen?
9. Were you just notified by the manufacturer that all your sculptures made of their new plastic may explode in ten minutes and they have already declared Chapter 11?
10. Do people avoid you because they are envious of your talent and good looks?
11. Are you still searching for your:

a. checkbook?

b. glasses?

c. wife/ husband / significant other?

d. something, but you can't remember what?

12. Do changes of season get you down, even
      when the change is for the better?

13. Are you consumed with regret?

If you can answer yes to seven or more of the test questions, you've suffered enough. Maybe more than enough. Maintain your present level, skip the next several paragraphs and go to the last one for your final test.

Answering affirmatively three to six of the questions suggests some work before success strikes. Add about a 30% dosage of stress and suffering and let's see how that does after, say, 60 days.

Is Museum Quality Work Eluding You Because You're Too Happy?

If you can say yes to less than three, you are not producing museum quality work because you are too happy. And happy, as you know, doesn't cut it. Work up to anguish gradually, but you will need the full load.

You are now at the stage where you may design a personal program of self-torture that will put you on the road to eventual greatness. Include at least two <u>required</u> miseries and three <u>optionals</u>** from the list below to your daily grind. Carefully observe any improvements you notice in your art and make periodic adjustments.

Required Miseries

1. Smile even though your heart is breaking...6 units.
2. Love your worst enemies...5 to 11 units, depending on enemy.
3. Include Brussels sprouts or liver with onions in your diet once a week...40 units.
4. Watch "Days of Our Lives" religiously until "they" come to haul you away...10 units per episode.
5. Try bending down and picking up some of the things you drop on the floor...1 unit per pickup. (Increase that to 28 units per if you don't bend your knees.)
6. Think the worst...10 units.
7. Abuse by others is OK, but self-abuse is best...6 units per self-criticism.

8. Think over what others say to you. There can always be a hidden, hurtful message...8 units per imagined insult.
9. Paint a Sistine Chapel ceiling while lying on your back for 5 years...128 units per year.

Optional Sufferings

1. Unrequited love...12 units
2. Cold showers...2 units.
3. Start a drastic weight-loss program at a Baskin & Robbins, and when the counterperson asks you what you will have, you say, "Nothing for me, thanks"...8 units.
4. Tell yourself that since things always run in groups of three, if you ruin four paintings in a row, you are simply starting on the next group of three...2 units.
5. Don't sell your exercycle at your next garage sale. Instead, use it a half hour each day without fail...3 units.
6. Imagine being condemned to watch all 90 episodes of "Victory at Sea" in one sitting... 3 units.

7. Listen to Barbara Streisand sing, "You Don't Send Me Flowers Anymore."...2 units per cry.
8. Turn on TV. Watch only the commercials for 4 hours. Go to bathroom or refrigerator during programs...7 units.
9. Think about all the things that are "just not the same anymore"...1.5 units per sigh.
10. Live in Los Angeles...6 units per commute.

Don't Settle For Mild Aggravation

Keep in mind that though you mustn't overdo, you also must never settle for a mild case of aggravation. It won't do the trick. Pain and suffering -- you've got to go for it. But don't expect immediate or permanent results. The correct dose of pain required to produce priceless paintings often also depends on the weight, height, age and intelligence *(how come you didn't mention THAT before?)* of the artist. Experiment.

Once you feel you carry between 70 to 80 depressnicks*** of agony, visit your nearest gallery. A trained gallery owner can tell immediately by looking at you --without even examining your art -- whether to recommend you increase the dosage or go on maintenance. He can also inform you when to expect significant improvements in your art.

** For the latest, most complete list of optional and required sufferings, see Nebish and Gornisht, pages 17 through 384, *So You Think You Have Troubles? You Don't Know the Meaning of Troubles!* Tsores Press, Philadelphia, PA.

*** 4.72 Imperial Depressnicks equal 1 International Angst. For the complete Depressnicks table, see Nebish and Gornisht, ibid.

Paid Advertisements

Used Art Supplies. I know what it's like when you're an artist just getting started and you're on a tight budget. That's why I decided to help fledgling artists by opening up the world's **first and only** store to sell **USED ART SUPPLIES**. I stock nearly everything you will need for painting, sculpture, even performance art, all under one roof! You can't imagine the **Savings**! You won't believe the **Bargains**! Here are just a few examples of the amazing buys waiting for you at **THE USED ART SUPPLIES EMPORIUM**:

- Stock up and save on **watercolor paper**. Most sheets have paintings of flowers, abandoned cars, boats and locomotives painted only on one side! The other side is blank and awaiting your touch! All brands and surfaces. Some were very expensive!
- Lots of **pre-stretched canvas**. We were lucky to find hundreds of these pre-painted canvasses carefully stored in closets, basements, even under beds. Mostly oils, some acrylics. They are easily painted over with your next masterpiece. Some are even still framed to save you $$$!
- I have hundreds of **tubes of paint**, many slightly squeezed. Some brands not made anymore! Some untouched tubes full of dried-up colors just waiting for a little water or thinner to work like new!
- **Hundreds of palettes**. A little scraping with an industrial sander will make them good as new. Dirt cheap!
- **Brushes, brushes, brushes**. Many with bristles intact. Some sables show slight moth damage but have lots of hair left. Some brush handles show tooth marks but that shouldn't affect results.
- **Are you a sculptor?** Here's great news! I have a large number of used sculptures, some figurative, some simply large blocks with engraved names and dates, like, "Born 1884 - Died 1929". But there's plenty of stone left to make smaller, better pieces with your creative talents. Sold AS-IS. Marble, granite, whatever. Buy by the ton and save!
- **Colored pencil bargains** for enthusiasts! Almost every color imaginable to draw those cute little rabbits, kitties and flowers. Many pencils almost full length. I even have metal extenders for the stubby ones so you don't hurt your nails. Also, some dried-up felt tip markers. Add some kind of thinner and watch them spring back to life.
- Lots of **performance art costumes**. Some good as new. Many have been rolled around on the floor a little and could use a cleaning.

Hundreds of other bargains too. Write for latest mimeographed catalog. **Flip Sturgis Used Art Supplies Emporium, Box EPA.**

Chapter 2

Episode number 497 in our exciting continuing TV Medidrama:

Artists' Hospital

where sick and dying paintings and sculpture are often saved, thanks to the modern miracle of reconstructive creativity

The crisis in the operating room!

(Scene: Crowded, busy hospital hallway. Hospital attendants and nurses rushing, two try to push through crowds with stretcher laden with cans of paint; people milling, shouting, talking, emergency-type pandemonium, "Get out of the way!", "Where can I find...," etc.., while loudspeaker blares).

LOUDSPEAKER

Stat! Emergency! Code Three! Dr. Brusque in surgery! Code Blue! Code Yellow! No! It's code Green plus a touch of Code Red, which makes a lovely, Warm Green Code. Call for Dr. Lautrec, extension 7747!

(Cut to waiting room. One family of four is sitting off to one side. Two people are standing. One is a tall, pretty, dark-haired, slim woman in jeans and a long, gray sweatshirt. Her hair is close-cropped and she has a ring in her nose. She speaks earnestly to a shorter, heavy-set, bald, bespectacled, young man with a long, scraggly brown beard.)

FERN

Phil. They've just got to save that painting!
Alger's put his heart and soul into that piece and it
could be his big break! It could also be a new
beginning for the two of us. I...I... Phil, I'm
carrying Alger's child!

PHIL

My God, Fern! What about Deliciosa Hamburger?
He's supposed to marry her tomorrow in the
Chapel at St. Anthony's!

FERN

He doesn't love her! He never has!

PHIL

But she's carrying three of his children!

FERN

I don't care if she's carrying twenty! He doesn't
love her. He told me that. He loves me and love

is everything. EVERYTHING! I know I couldn't live without Alger and he couldn't live without me. Oh...this wait is so awful... When in God's name will they repair his painting?

(Cut to operating room. Chief Art Doctor, old Dr. Brusque is bent over a painting on the operating table. A handsome, dark-haired assistant art doctor and three art nurses surround the table. All are dressed in green gowns, pants, caps and masks.)

FIRST ART NURSE

(Whisper) If anyone can pull this one off, old Dr. Brusque can. He's the best I've ever watched. Look at him work with that Number 7 palette knife! God! It's like poetry!

ART NURSE HASSENFELDER

(Whisper) Yes, I agree. But you know, Kelly, this is my first operation under Brusque, and I _am_ a little nervous. I just want to do my very best!

DR. BRUSQUE

Stop that cadiddling over there and pay attention. I've got enough on my mind without a lot of namby pambying. Let's get on with it. NUMBER 10 HOG BRISTLE FILBERT!

(Nurse slaps brush in old Dr. Brusque's open, gloved hand. Brusque takes it, looks up, white with anger).

DR. BRUSQUE

You fool! That's not a number 10 hog bristle filbert! Don't you know the difference between a number 10 hog bristle and a number 10 BRIGHT? I want you out of here. I WANT HER OUT OF HERE!

ART NURSE HASSENFELDER

(She cries, says between sobs.) Please, Dr. Brusque. I can do it! I know I can. I've studied so hard and this is my first real art operation under you. I know all our instruments perfectly but I

was just a little nervous. I'll show you. I can do it perfectly! Please give me another chance!

DR BRUSQUE

(Apoplectic with rage. Shouting.) I WANT HER OUT OF HERE! I WILL NOT BE SURROUNDED BY INCOMPETENTS! I WON'T...

ASSISTANT ART DOCTOR FESTER

(Soothingly) Relax, Paul. Paul! Calm down. You're going to have a heart attack if you keep that up! Give the kid a break, Paul... *(starts to sing calmingly, "When You Wish Upon a Star.")*

(Cut to commercial in laboratory setting. Announcer appears in white, scientist-type laboratory coat. He speaks...)

ANNOUNCER

Welcome to the world of Winsor and Newton. The two most famous names in paint. *(Walks around actors who pretend to grind paint.)* Here's how we make the finest paint using the finest ingredients. *(Pats shoulder of one actor.)* But the best news is just in time for those paintings you're just itching to do at the seashore. W & N is introducing four new and exclusive beach colors! Dry Sand. Wet Sand. Dry Rocks and Wet Rocks. Those colors are available in 5, 15 and 37 milliliter tubes and in 5-gallon drums for those really big canvasses. Be sure to visit your nearest art dealer, look for those new introductions, and stock up on Winsor Newton Colors. They're the best!

(Cut to art studio in upper north side of Metropolis. Floor is littered with old tubes of paint, paper, scraps of sandwiches, etc. Young man with palette and brush in hand is standing dejected before easel holding half-finished portrait. Heavy set woman with long hair flowing down past her waist is dressed in floor length dirty flowered muumuu. She speaks.)

AGNESS

I don't want to hurt your feelings, Florid, but it's time to send it to Artists' Hospital.

FLORID

Over my dead body, Agness! I know I can get it right if I have a little more time. I think it doesn't look right because there must be something small I've missed.

AGNESS

Florid! You've been working on that painting of Little Dorit for over twelve years now. You have paint three inches thick on her nose and you must know it's still off to one side. All Mrs. Thurbill wants is a likeness. We're out of food and nothing's coming in. Believe me, give it up, Florid, and send it to the hospital! They'll fix it. They'll make it right and we can get on with our lives.

FLORID

(Tears well up in his eyes as camera goes in for close-up. Covers face with hands. Takes hands away. Face now covered with paint.)

God, Agness, you know I've worked my ass off on this one. Sometimes they come so easy. This one's just been real hard. Maybe I just been kidding myself that I'm a real artist. I'm no damn good!

AGNESS

Agness goes to him, holds him.) Not good enough? You're the best, Florid. They don't come any better. You've just had a tough break...and there are times *(she looks out dirty window)*...when we all need a little help from something... or somebody...

FLORID

You're right. Yeah. You're right. I've been a fool to hang on this long. It's time to get a life, time to get a handle on things, to move along, to something or other. Know what I mean?

AGNESS

I'll call the hospital.

(Cut to announcer in white coat for final commercial. Close-up, honest, sincere face, then dissolve to scenes from upcoming show.)

ANNOUNCER

Thank you for joining us for this exciting episode of Artists' Hospital. Do you think the ambulance will arrive in time to save Florid's nose? Will old Chief Art Surgeon Dr. Brusque think it over and allow Nurse Hassenfelder back into his operating room? Will Dr. Fester break into another song? Will Fern marry Alger? What will happen to Deliciosa? You'll surely want to stay tuned right here for the next heart-wrenching episode. In the meantime, just remember: Winsor Newton Paint is THE BEST PAINT for artists everywhere!

(Cut to three tubes of Winsor Newton paint. They squeeze each other. Streams of red, yellow and blue paint emerge, converge into intricate patterns that end by spelling out logo for company.)

(Dissolve to 11 o'clock News.)

Please Patronize Our Advertisers

Chapter 3

Starving Artist's Cookbook

or how to find healthy, low cost meals free or on a limited budget

Maybe you are doing protest-type paintings or works with a lot of dirty words or

"Hey boss. How about painting something
in tuna?"

explicit obscene sculpture and there is little or no demand just yet. Or perhaps you are just starting out and there seems to be an unpleasant distance between available galleries, your income and your stomach. Yet, you still have to eat. For you to remain at your easel, it's important to maintain your health with some sort of free or cheap balanced meals. Let's also start with the assumption that since so much of your energy and waking time is spent thinking about art, you don't even want to take time to cook.

Gallery Openings. Be There!

Your first project is to check newspapers and galleries for gallery openings. More and more, I find regular gallery openings occurring on, say, the first Thursday of every month. It would be better for you if these things were spaced out; but, at least make it a point every month to visit several galleries on Thursdays.

Gallery openings often provide an excellent source of protein in the form of cheese and sometimes beef, plain or in sandwiches. Sometimes vegetables are available for grazing -- like carrots, radishes, celery, plus dip, which is usually sour cream (another excellent source of protein) with added flavorings like onion. Make sure you get plenty of protein and carbohydrates to keep up your strength.

Often cheap wine is available. Drink but don't overindulge. You don't want to look greedy and you may also have to remember where you live.

Look Like You Might Buy Something

I find it best when attending gallery openings to appear as if you might buy something.

At all costs, avoid sticking your nose right up against a painting to see how an artist does brushstrokes. That's a dead giveaway you're an artist looking for a free meal.

Try to look different from time to time so you won't be too easy to remember. Wear a clean shirt or a dress if you have one, or borrow one from a friend.

Change styles, comb your hair, grow a beard, add a wig. Ask questions like, "How much is *'Blue Dot in White Field'*?", or "Do you take checks?", or "Do you offer payment plans?" Keep them guessing. Gallery owners aren't stupid and if they find enough artists taking up floor space, they may stop serving food, and then where will we be?

In fact, some galleries have already eliminated food at openings and I wouldn't personally give them the time of day.

But Wait. There's Good News!

A relatively new but regular source of sustenance for artists may be found in supermarkets and big discount warehouse-type stores. Here, servers at tables are providing everything from breakfast cereals to main courses as free samples.

This type of giving occurs on specific days during the week, like Thursdays and Saturdays, and it behooves the artist to jot down and remember these dates to participate in the events.

Be Sure to Push a Loaded Cart Like Everyone Else

When you do choose to attend out of hunger, be sure to push a cart like everyone else.

Fill it nicely with boxes of soap, breakfast cereals, canned foods, candy and the like so you don't look like a schnorer. You can always unload those items following your repast when you are pleasantly satiated.

When sampling, be friendly but not too familiar or easily remembered. Always take two or three servings at a time, offering a flippant, "I don't know where my wife / husband is, but I want her (him) to try this!" On a return visit, add, "She (he) really loved this _____ (name of product) and asked for more!" Add light or slightly embarrassed laughter. ALWAYS ask in WHICH AISLE you might find the product you've sampled because that makes the demonstrator feel worthwhile.

There are other non-artistic events, but these often call for you to belong to something or donate money and if you were going to donate anything, it would be to your own private charity--your stomach.

Sponge Off Friends

The next choice is to sponge off friends. Not artist friends -- that's like sharing a lot of nothing. Choose friends who know how to fill a refrigerator. Try not to be your usual negative or disagreeable self. You'll need to keep lots of friends so you won't have to hit up the same ones all the time.

Finally, invite yourself over for dinner to parents' or relatives' homes. Be complimentary, eat heartily, appear to enjoy yourself immensely and ask what they're going to do with the leftovers if they don't ask you first. Of course, you have plenty of room in <u>your</u> refrigerator.

Become an Entrepreneur

After exhausting all the above, we're down to bedrock. First, do you have some money? Because here we're faced with BUYING! If you are short, you can go into business with a Safeway shopping cart collecting and redeeming bottles. Many street people have become prosperous entrepreneurs by redeeming hundreds of soft drink bottles and cans at two to five cents each!

Best time for working the bottle business is around lunchtime when office workers are casting them into the trash after they finish their sandwiches and carrots. But move fast. There are other artists out there plus some other real savvy professionals working the street.

Now let's say you have some money. I suggest three cheap, time-proven recipes. The only requirements are a refrigerator and some cooking facilities, like a can of Sterno.

TUNA SUPREME
1 can cheap tuna
1 can Campbell Mushroom Soup.
Mix and heat. Spoon over toast or crackers.
Serves 3 days. Don't share or it won't last 3 days.

CHIPPED BEEF EDUARDE
1 can Chipped Beef (preferably on sale)
1 can Campbell Mushroom Soup
Mix and heat. Spoon over toast or crackers.
Serves 4 days because it doesn't taste that good.

SPAM de CANNES
Open a can of Spam
Eat some with lots of catsup or mustard.
Serves two weeks or much longer. You may never want to finish it.

Paid Advertisements

Be a Court Painter! We represent several Monarchs and Potentates in certain countries who are looking for court artists who will make them and their families look good in paint. Many portraits may require considerable artistic license. Failure will not be easily tolerated and the consequences of an unfavorable likeness can be harsh. However, artists interested in selling out for money, travel, power and a life of luxury will find any one of our locations an ideal opportunity to prostitute their art. Write: **Royal Road to Art, Box CBS**.

Learn to Paint While You Sleep! Now, you can put almost every bedtime hour to work and become the painter you never thought you could be. Pop one of our instructional tapes into the Sominor and 20 minutes after you hit the pillow, you will learn to paint better instead of wasting time counting sheep. Just buy taped lessons by favorite artist-teachers, and simply rent the Sominor player. If you are not completely satisfied after buying and using six tapes, return the Sominor to us. No questions asked. Sorry. No refunds on used tapes. Write for list of tapes, prices and SPECIAL DISCOUNTS. **Sominor, Box ZZZ**.

Charles Reid : Can you teach me to paint like you do? Willing to trade antique farm tools and other implements for lessons. **Ralph, Box 888**

Help Wanted : Position open to right young man or woman. Must be good fast painter able to paint at a variety of locations, willing to work day or night. Experienced in all mediums. Must like people. Materials and special truck provided. Immediate opening on night shift. Write to Shlep, **Emergency Art Service, Box BB.**

Tulip Time : Tour and paint in beautiful Holland this year! Visit Schraachthoven, the village time forgot. See the recently discovered 16th century studio of Schraacht, once world renowned portrait painter, friend of Rembrandt. Tour studio as he left it untouched over 300 years ago! Learn little-known painting tips. Copy world's first portrait price list devised by this famous artist. Fly with famed pilot, "Crash" Wilson from New York via Clip Aire. One-night stay and play in Copenhagen. Horse-drawn cart through Holland. Side trips, paint included, just bring your favorite brush. **Write Tulip Time Travel, Box L.**

**Bob paints portraits with the
ugliness removed.**

Bob's Portraits of Beauty!

By Bob Sodgrass, Artist

Hell. I know most of you take terrible pictures.

Isn't it true? Every time a camera is aimed your way, and you don't duck fast enough, you just know the results will make you look like something a dog has been chewing on. Yet, you would like to have the world remember you as you might have looked if your folks hadn't been so ugly and passed on their worst features to you.

Well, that's where *Portraits by Bob* comes to the rescue! Just mail me a photo of you, even out of focus, and a photo of the person you would like to have resembled if you had had a sporting chance. Then leave it up to me. When your BOB'S PORTRAIT OF BEAUTY arrives and hangs on your wall or sits on your piano or is held on your refrigerator by those cute little magnets, your family will be awestruck and green with envy.

Be Remembered For The Inner You

Those slimeball in-laws of yours will never again be able to point to your picture. guffaw and say that the worst features of their grandchildren came from <u>your side</u> of the family. No sir!

Seen through my miracle portrait, you will show them the inner beauty that is you! And when they've gone bye-bye (if you catch my drift) the next generation will think of you the way you want to be thought of. They won't know any better. You have MY WORD on that!

So, don't just sit there waiting for another wrinkle or a zit. Send your photos plus $99 by money order or check today to:

Bob's Portraits Of Beauty

Bob Sodgrass, Prop.

c/o Meyer's Fish & Feed
Box 7, Slurp, Oregon 97772.

Chapter 4

Leonardo DaVinci, Father Of Computer-Generated Art

Most people know that Leonardo DaVinci designed the Weed Eater and the first

flying machine, just two products of his ingenious
mind. Yet, unless one delves deep into the
archives, he is unaware that in 1514, five years
before his death, he also designed the first
computer capable of generating art.

At least, that's what I learned by coming
across a doctoral thesis by a Girolamo Libri in the
archives of Milan Technical School, where I
served for ten years as Professor of Crosshatch
Shading.

Libri points out that the computer may have
been crude by today's standards, but was quite
advanced for its time. After all, his so-called
smart neighbors were still trying to figure out if
the world was round. Leonardo's machine was
powered by a hand crank (an assistant was
necessary) and a series of rubber bands built inside
a rather large wooden device. The keyboard, of
course, was rudimentary and presented the greatest
challenge when multiplying or dividing by Roman
numerals.

Comes Too Late For Mona Lisa

Unfortunately, this invention came too late
for his painting of the Mona Lisa. Leonardo was

"Can we have a little
Gioconda smile, please."

never satisfied with that painting, especially the time he spent fussing over her expression. He once told a friend that if he had used his marvelous computer, he could have finished it in under five years (1503 to 1507) and maybe got the smile right. "Perhaps something more natural," he considered, "with some pretty white teeth showing."

He is reputed to have done only two computer-generated pieces including "Francesco Flying with DaVinci Flying Machine." It was produced on location as Francesco took off and plunged to his death using Leonardo's winged construction.* It created quite a flap at the time, and the painting technique, which centered on a large blurred figure, never found favor with the Borgias or any of the other collectors of his work.

Greatest Painting Lost

Sadly, his greatest computer-generated painting, the "Affirmation of the Ambrogio," is lost to us. Rumor has it that it was stolen by the Nazis in WW II and now hangs somewhere in an

*Following this first test flight, Leonardo replaced the model 6.0 with the 6.0A which had greater lift and safer landing characteristics.

obscure Siberian museum.

Actually, computer-generated art was never a great success. Most buyers preferred something done by hand which took one to three years to complete and somehow seemed more valuable. Guido Gallucci, one of Leonardo's favorite pupils and successor, never could get the computer to work right and it fell into disuse. Parts were removed to be used in early model dishwashers and vacuum cleaners.

Today's computers are really only the latest development built upon Leonardo's design. The rubber bands have, of course, been replaced by micro chips and electricity. The box is neither made of oak nor does it take up two large rooms and require two people to operate. But the basic idea hasn't changed that much.

Although the technique can now accomplish marvelous things, computer-generated art has not seriously invaded the two- to forty-million-dollar fine-art market. Today's art collectors still prefer to pay top dollar for hands-on fine art especially if the artist is dead and was French.

Paid Advertisements

Chapter 5

Emergency Art Service

I didn't get to sleep until about TWO in the morning. Something on my mind, I guess.

When minutes count! The night crew on the move!

Fifteen minutes after I hit the snore button --
wouldn't you know it!-- my boss at
EMERGENCY ART SERVICE calls and says,
"We need you for an emergency!"

I had just put in a rough day and I snarled
"What's wrong with the night crew?" They are all
out on other emergencies he told me, and this case
was right down my alley. He promised a little
something extra if I did the job...like a little
surprise in the old pay envelope.

I wrote down the name and address of the
customer and fell out of bed, groggy as a swollen
python digesting a missionary. I lumbered into
my uniform -- painter's smock, flowing red scarf
and black tam with our famous insignia. Fully
awake now, I jumped into our panel truck with its
gigantic, illuminated red plastic paint brush with
brilliant yellow handle. I reached for the siren,
changed my mind and turned on the flashing red
emergency light instead. Then I slammed into
first and burned rubber. Luckily, there wasn't any
traffic at that hour because our motto is "IF WE
DON'T GET TO YOUR HOUSE IN 30
MINUTES, THE PAINTING IS FREE."

I ground to a halt minutes later on the red gravel circular driveway fronting the imposing Flemsley mansion, a modern "Destructivist" design. I rushed to the door, where my ring was answered by a recorded trumpet trio playing "Fanfare to the Common Man" by Copeland, and before the last notes faded, the door swung open. In place of the haughty butler I expected, I was greeted by a sweaty, heavyset, balding man in striped blue pajamas and red silk robe.

I introduced myself and tried to shake his hand. It was so wet with perspiration, I slipped off but he caught me before I fell.

"I'm Horace Flemsley," he groaned, his breathing labored, "and thank God you're here. My wife, Edna, is driving me and everyone else *Meshuge* about getting a painting to match her crazy color scheme. She's looked everywhere and we're at our wits' end!"

He stopped for a moment to catch his breath and rushed on. "All the servants have bolted and we've been without help or sleep for I don't remember how long, and for the life of me, I can't get her calmed down."

I hardly had time to say, "I can take care of that!" before he wetly grabbed my arm. Quickly, he pulled me through the huge entryway, down a long hallway into a massive ballroom -- our steps reverberating on the polished marble floor -- shouting as we ran, "Edna! Edna! You can stop crying! Help's coming!"

I Offer Soothing Words

Edna, dressed in a Lagerfeld silver metallic bed frock was lying face down on a multi-colored floral red chintz sofa near the great French doors. She was crying uncontrollably. I walked softly toward her, remembering how we had learned in our training program to handle excitable customers. With soothing words, I managed to calm her down. Flemsley watched as I stroked her hair, and between sobs she said, "I didn't know where to turn. I simply CANNOT find a painting that goes with this cherry red floral couch, lemon rug and blue floral walls. Is there ANYTHING you can do? I just KNOW I'll go INSANE!"

I don't know how many times I've heard that before. "Ma'am, that's why I'm here," I quietly murmured. "May I set up my easel in here? "

She nodded.

I walked to the truck and returned with my easel, paints, brushes, a variety of frames and a tarp for the floor.

"Do you mind if we watch you create?" Mr. Flemsley asked.

"Of course not," I said. "I think it's so with it for you to FEEL the work really brings out the deep inner you as I build the painting."

I examined the color scheme critically from this angle and that, sort of like a golfer checking out the green before putting. I set up my easel and equipment and whipped up an abstract that included the primary colors in less than eighteen minutes.

Edna was so excited she danced like a child with her first Barbie Doll. I brushed back a tear as Horace enfolded her in his strong, sweaty arms.

"How can we ever thank you enough?" the two asked of me.

I whispered hoarsely, my voice shaking with the deep love and affection I felt for my new friends, "Visa or Discover. We take both."

I wrote out the charge and gave them their receipt. After we had hugs, the Flemsleys gave me a fond good night. I wrapped up my things and took them out to the truck.

I am deeply moved

I knew I was tired and would have to get up early in the morning to start my shift all over again, but I was deeply moved by a wonderfully warm feeling. As I hit the sack, I remembered Edna's last words to me:

"Thank you and thank all those who also stand and serve the public above and beyond the call of duty at EMERGENCY ART SERVICE."

Paid Advertisements

Rent or Buy the Sturdily Electric Tube Squeezer! Are you wasting half your paint and half your money hand-squeezing tubes of expensive paint? Are you using a manual squeezer and throwing away your precious time when you could be using it to create priceless masterpieces? Then it's time to turn to the IMPROVED Sturdily "Python" Electric Floor Model Tube Squeezer! Gets every last drop of paint out of every tube in seconds! The new Sturdily "Python" can't catch your fingers like some competing electrics, is even safe for children with careful adult supervision. The Sturdily sensor stops the squeeze at the right moment before the cap blows. Endorsed on TV! Only $89.95 at art dealers. Ask to see a demonstration today!

To Museum Directors: I have a collection of watercolors by my late husband, C.J. Lemming, which I would like to donate to a worthy art museum. These paintings include scenes of Camp Wichiwheree, coastal reveries (he loved the ocean) and works showing our children and grandchildren at play in our back yard. A special favorite painting of mine is one of our daughter at her first tap-dancing lesson. My husband never sold any of them and before he was lost at sea, told me that he hoped they would someday grace the walls of the Metropolitan Museum. I thank God that C. J. left me his entire collection along with the Lemming fortune. Therefore I would like to donate his paintings as a permanent collection and also a check for $2,000,000 to the institution which accepts his paintings. I am not sure how to go about this bequest. Is there a museum interested? **Ethel, Box BVD**.

Interpret your dreams in art : Discover life-transforming wisdom in your dreams and paint it (them). Course by mail tells what to eat before bedtime to have great paintable dreams. Diet includes lots of chocolate ice cream, the more the better, chocolate chip cookies, plus other favorites to help you dream in vivid colors. Unique opportunity. Your dreams guaranteed to be different from other artists. We dare you to compare! Start today on this integrative psychotherapeutic art form. Great for showing life passages. **Nittyditty Institute, Box 711.**

Joan : I didn't mean what I said about your paintings. Kids miss you terribly. Please come home. **Paul, Box 9C**

Chapter 6

Portraits by Schraacht

Major Credit Cards Welcome

Recently while driving through a tiny Dutch hamlet, I found myself literally "off the map," completely lost. I stopped at a farmhouse

**The vision which greeted me
is almost impossible to describe.**

for directions. Although I don't speak a word of Dutch, the Dutch farmer and I were able to keep up a fair conversation. We used hand signs, body movements, a few common words, scratched naughty pictures in the dirt with twigs, and painted little faces on our hands to make funny expressions. We discussed routes, the weather, tulips and other matters of local and international interest. In the midst of this conversation, that white-haired old local farmer paused and searched my face but couldn't find anything he had lost. Yet, he wanted to tell me something special...a secret only the inhabitants of the village knew.

Village Home To Famous Painter

"You are very fortunate," he sighed, moving very close to me. "This village was once home to a famous, but forgotten portrait painter. Unfortunately, the artist and our village are no longer recognized," he gestured.

"Then, what a stroke of luck it is that I have come here of all places, not knowing I was lost on sacred ground," I flashed with my arms and left leg. "I am also a painter of portraits!"

He was stunned. I propped him up against a tree while he regained his composure.

"Thank you," he signaled with a flare pistol, adding, "You are our first visiting artist in over 300 years, I believe. Did you know that this is the very place where Schraacht, the 17th century master portrait painter, lived? Rembrandt, along with many other masters, often paid many guilders to attend his summer workshops, you know."

After a brief pause, he scratched in the moist earth, "Would you like to see his studio? It hasn't been touched since he lived there, over three centuries ago." Naturally, having done a portrait or two myself, you can imagine my answer!

I quickly followed my guide down a little dirt road at the edge of the village. We soon came upon an ancient hand-lettered sign almost completely hidden by tall grass and accumulated dirt. I pulled away some taller grass. The legend, still faintly readable, announced:

"Portraits by Schraacht, Since 1638
MAJOR CREDIT CARDS WELCOME."

What a find, I thought as I hurried toward the crumbling, thatch-covered cottage beyond the sign. With the aid of my companion, I pushed open the stubborn, vine-covered door.

The vision that greeted me is almost impossible to describe. Covered in thick dust and cobwebs were easels in every corner of the main room exhibiting Schraacht portraits. Some pictured headless bodies clothed in the rich furnishings of the very wealthy. The heads would be painted in later, I was told by hand signs, when the sitter chose the body and elaborate costume preferred. (Now, there's an idea for you!)

But what caught my eye was a sign translated in five languages including Esperanto (in which I'm expert) prominently displayed near the door, sprinkled with soft light from a dust-covered window. I was thunderstruck! To my knowledge, this was the first portrait price list ever published! It read:

PORTRAITS BY SCHRAACHT
...since 1638

- Full figure....75 guilders

- Half figure....57 guilders
- Weight reduction, per pound....6 driblicks
- Lines, wrinkles and warts eliminated....10 driblicks
- Extra hair added, as desired....15 driblicks
- Head only........20 guilders, 10 driblicks
- General beautification, perky noses, penetrating or twinkling eyes, strong jaws, full lips, youth reclaimed...3 guilders per pound of paint
- Rings, necklaces, jewelry and elaborate costumes... price depends on size and quality as chosen from our extensive Spiegel catalog
- Hand in pocket or hidden.......free
- One hand, all five fingers showing......13 driblicks
- Two hands, all ten fingers painted...1 guilder

BACKGROUNDS

- Suggestive and abstract....1 guilder, 7 driblicks
- Home interiors, fussy ornate structures, objects requiring a lot of perspective.....4 to 7 guilders
- Mystical symbols, angels, etc., each....12 guilders

GUILD GROUP-PORTRAITS
A SPECIALTY

- Prominent figures for front row....69 guilders
- Inferior persons (but "real comers") for second and third rows, may not be exactly facing the viewer....39 guilders

Sorry. No rush jobs.
No weekend deadlines.
Best to call for an appointment.

Here was a master with honesty and integrity who wasn't afraid to be up front with his clients. What courage to spell out his prices in advance, including the extra charge for hands! (We all know how hard fingers can be to paint!)

I copied that price list with a view toward using it in my practice but am only too happy to share with my fellow artists. Naturally, some minor adjustments may be necessary, depending on your area, clientele and the current exchange rate of the driblick.

"Will you please hold the picture still,
Miss Perkins?"

We'll Do All or Part of the Painting for You!

71

Want your painting to look like something done by Rembrandt or Wyeth or Norman Rockwell or Sorolla or some other artist living or dead?   And you want to give it to a loved one as a present or maybe you even want to sell it and make a lot of money?

But you don't think you can even draw a straight line, let alone paint your way out of a paper bag?

We'll Even Paint in Your Signature!

Don't sweat it. Now you can do something about your lack of talent. Just send us a photo you want copied into a painting and we'll paint it in the exact style of any master you choose. We'll even paint in your signature in any form and color you prefer. And we promise we'll never tell anyone you didn't do it yourself. Even if it winds up selling for a million dollars and finds a home in the Metropolitan Museum of Art.

As for prices on our paintings...we practically give them away just to keep busy. Mail that photo today and name the artist whose style you most admire, along with $5 and we'll do the rest.

BROADVIEW HOME for the Artistically Insane

7 Straitjacket Square, Venus, CA. 94221

Visitors are always welcome, but please call first.

**With the first notes of Humoresque,
they became tame as kittens.**

Chapter 7

Lost letter reveals:

How Animals Learn to Hold Long Poses While Edward Hicks Paints "Peaceable Kingdom"

Who hasn't asked himself at

least once, "How did Edward Hicks get the creatures he painted to hold long poses without eating him or each other while he worked?"

Yesterday, I DISCOVERED THE ANSWER! It was among some garage sale items I purchased for $11, including a priceless Vermeer, some solid gold candlesticks AND a letter written in 1885 by Hicks to his cousin Billy Bob Flemish, describing his painting process! (One can often find real bargains at a garage sale!)

Now we know that Hicks first tried adding a mild sedative to the feed for his models, but results were disappointing. It seemed to put the animals to sleep and, worse luck(!), they slept on their backs with their paws and hooves in the air during the painting session. Hicks writes Billy Bob, "I feel their positions lack excitement and may not appeal to the general public!"

Tries Painting Inside Special Cage

Later, he tried using circus trainers while he painted in a cage similar to the type used to film man-eating shark TV shows. Again, although the procedure kept the animals in place, painting in a cage was uncomfortable and the flashing whips upset his models. They made no attempt to hide their obvious anger and contempt.

Savage Beasts Soothed by Music

Then one night at a concert, he remembered the adage that "music soothes the savage beast" and, "I came up with a unique idea!" he exclaimed in his letter! The next morning, when he had his animals take their places on the set, and the carnivores were estimating the taste-value of their nearest neighbor, he signaled a violinist he had hired to play "Humoresque." Miraculously, with the first notes of the melody, the beasts became tame as kittens. Soon they developed strong friendships among themselves which they maintained to their dying days. Hicks delightedly painted this tranquil scene to his heart's content. It made his fortune and he did at least 25 more versions for which his animals happily posed.

And that's how I came to know the secret of "The Peaceable Kingdom."

Through his letter, I also learned that upon completion of the series, the animals, now close friends, decided not to return to forest and field, but to remain together and form a theatrical troupe, called the *"Peacemakers."* A theatrical manager named Henderson or Hmndrsn (the writing here is illegible) was hired to develop an act for them which became the rage of Europe and America for nearly fourteen years.

The act opened with the orchestra playing *Humoresque.* As the curtains parted, a single blue spotlight followed each animal as it entered the stage, stopped stage-center to bow to the audience, then turned to take its place in the giant living tableaux of the *Peaceable Kingdom!* Audiences were ecstatic!

Animals Add "Hoofing" to Act

In time, as paying customers grew fewer and less enthusiastic, some of the members of the troupe introduced singing and tap dancing which they called "hoofing."

When bookings finally dried up, and the *Peacemakers* found themselves penniless and stranded in Joseph, Oregon, Mr. Hicks contacted his manager and had the act brought to Attlesboro, Pennsylvania. There he had a home built for his aging four-legged (and winged) friends which he named *Peaceable Home*. It was on these grounds that the beasts of his paintings spent their declining years. The home was finally closed when the last survivor, Abner, lead wolf, lay down to rest and rejoin the famous troupe.

Paid Advertisements

Chapter 8

Scouts! Earn Merit Badges for Art!

My troop Number 145 is
composed entirely of youngsters who come to us

**Flem gets a major installation in a
Big Apple Gallery**

from dysfunctional families. In fact, one of our requirements for membership is that they do come from families that dysfunction or do not function real well, if you know what I mean.

And yet, in spite of their unfortunate home lives, most of my scouts have developed into strong-minded, healthy and alert young men thanks to acquiring an intense appreciation of art. Art is the backbone of our craft program and almost all our boys have earned numerous merit badges in that field toward their First Class and Eagle rank.

Scouts Required To Explain Concepts In Complete Sentences

I would like to tell you about a few of them, omitting their last names, of course. But before I do, I must tell you that the rules require that the scout not only paint or sculpt or whatever in the style studied, but must understand the concept and explain it to the judge or judges in complete sentences, including subjects and verbs.

First, there is Randy, whose parents are both psychologists. They sit around and look at him and each other and say things like, "How do you feel about that?" or, "As I understand it, what you're saying is..." or, "I hear you." That kind of thing.

Randy Tries Kinetic Abstraction

Once he had passed his rudimentary tests for scouting, which consists of rubbing two matches together to make fire, Randy didn't know what to do with himself until he dove in and took an avid interest in art.

Randy earned his badge for painting in the "Kinetic Abstract" mode. The judge, a gallery owner, was enthusiastic as he watched Randy leap into the air, fall to the floor and rub himself in paint, flop around and smash the paint to the canvas, then jump up, leap again and so on. Still lathered in paint from head to foot, he explained the meaning of the style and why he chose to paint that way. Isn't that quite something for a 13-year old boy from a dysfunctional family? Needless to say, he earned his badge with honors.

Slug's was a different case entirely. His mother is a transvestite and his father is a cross dresser. Slug's problem was not knowing who to turn to or to whom he was turning.

He took to scouting like an egg to hot water. In a few short weeks, he developed an interest in art and was awarded two merit badges; our first scout to win two in art in only six weeks. His first badge was awarded for a series of very large minimalist paintings which Slug did entirely in black asphalt on canvas. He called the series "Street." When queried by the judge, he explained, "It says everything. It says nothing." The judge was thunderstruck and died right there on the spot after making the presentation.

Slug Earns Badge For White Umbrellas

The presiding judge attending the second merit badge ceremony for Slug made sure he was electrically grounded before the demonstration to avoid the jolt meted out to the prior judge. For this major work, Slug chose to display a series of white painted umbrellas fastened to white boards. Since each umbrella was broken, torn, or had parts missing, Slug described the style as "Fragmented Durealism" (his term, meaning *two* realistic connected broken tokens of art). His explanation and dissertation so confounded Judge Albie Butterfeet, that he awarded Slug two gold oak leaves to go with the badge, the highest award attainable for art merit badges.

My next example of youngsters picking up quickly on art, is Flem. Flem didn't fit in well with the other boys and we were afraid we would have to kick his butt out of the troop. As a child, he was abandoned regularly on the front steps of St. Anthony's on Alder Street by one family after another. The last family which tried to abandon him was stopped at the door by Father Ribaldo and told that they would go to Hell if they tried that again.

Experience Depresses Parents

That experience made his last set of parents very depressed because they couldn't agree which Hell to go for -- keeping Flem or hoping for the best in the final damnation. It was from this black atmosphere that Flem came to us, and he in effect shrouded us in his gloom. But then, one meeting he was all smiles. He had discovered art. He was a new youth!

Sculpting became his passion and merit badges came thick and fast. His first badge was won for a series of soft sculptures which looked exactly like dirty old flour sacks. He saw this work as "Pillsbury XXX Expressionism," a kind of "Neo-Geo-Sumo Wrestlingism." The judge for this badge was the director of the museum, and she was ecstatic. On the basis of that work, she gave him a one-person show at the museum, and for that he won his second merit badge for art.

NY Galleries Vie For Flem Show!

In this show, Flem produced a two-room installation of dynamic proportions, filling one entire room with toilet paper donated by friends, family and a local supermarket. Some paper was left in rolls dipped in various colors, much of it unrolled and strung among wires and forms and hanging from light fixtures. In the main gallery, Flem arranged shoes, stuffed toys, a few transitional rolls of toilet paper, sacks, boom boxes playing rap music and multi-colored streamers all hanging from the ceiling. In addition, the floor was covered with fire-retardant straw, three old mattresses painted with Glidden "Harvest Gold" house paint, wrapping paper, used paper towels from a nearby motel, Kleenex, old newspapers, sacks, garbage cans filled with broken bottles, plastic junk, cans of partly decomposed tuna fish and eight incomplete mannequins in need of repair.

As young Flem explained, the entire abstraction of real images virtually attacked every sense of the viewer. Several members of the vast audience were so overwhelmed they had to be rushed to waiting ambulances. Nothing the museum had ever attempted before made such a powerful impact on our town. At the merit badge award ceremony, two gallery owners from New York vied with each other for the opportunity to represent Flem with a major show in the Big Apple.

Could Give Other Examples

There are many more examples I might give you of the tremendous impact art has had on the boys in our troop. And remember, our boys have had two strikes against them because they come from dysfunctional families. Imagine what successful boys working with full decks can do in your troops. But the experiences of my three boys may be enough to give you scoutmasters some ideas on how to further the careers of your young scouts by helping them grasp the challenge of earning merit badges in art.

Write Today!

For those of you who are unaware of the many art merit badges available, ask about the complete list. These include badges for "Abstract Expressionism," "Primevalism," "Hedonistic Impracticism," "Neo-Geo Ablutionism," and even "Realisticism," plus over 73 other style categories.

If you would like a complete list of the potential badges which may be earned, and Rule Booklet LLBENE, write as I did to the scouting headquarters in your area. Tell them you heard the good news about the Scoutart Program and want to get started! If you tell them your scouts come from dysfunctional families, you will get a quicker reply.

The Gold Picture-Hanger-Ring Award
Ceremony is most impressive.

Chapter 9

Intense Training Key to Successful Art Gallery Operation

Many artists think that anyone who wants to be around art can easily open an art gallery. NOT TRUE! Today, to be successful, most attend the Mecca of schools, the New York Art Gallery Training Institute (NYAGTI) on Madison Avenue. There they are given a concentrated three week course on how to come in out of the rain, gallery-wise, that is.

Applicants soon learn the differences between mediums which is so important to effective gallery operation. They discover the best way to be certain it's a watercolor is by licking a finger and rubbing off some of the paint. They also quickly learn that an oil painting is usually shiny, and has a texture one can feel by stroking or running a nail over the image. One helpful rule applicants memorize during the course is, "If you lick the paint and the paint won't come off and it's not an oil painting, it probably is a print." Perhaps that's a good rule for all of us to remember.

Intense classes teach how to knowingly squint through slides by pointing them toward the light, take Polaroid pictures to mail to prospects, and learn to tell the difference between potential customers and artists. (The ones who put their faces to within an inch of the painting to "see how it was done" are artists.)

Candidates Learn to Never Get Pushy

Casual indifference and self-control are essential to graduation. Here the applicant learns NEVER to get pushy. Such tactics as confidentially suggesting to a customer that "we can't keep this artist in stock," or "I strongly urge you to buy it now, because it may not be here when you return," or "I believe it's sold, but wait a moment and I'll make sure I can save it for you," are held in contempt. Any miscreant convicted of such abuse is ousted in shame, forced to clean out his locker, march before the student body to the beat of muffled drums, and take the first Greyhound bus home.

Applicants Learn to Rise Early

Each applicant is required to jump out of bed by 10 am, have a leisurely breakfast, and make telephone calls for an hour before lunch. This is one of the more taxing aspects of the job, and early risers who can't adjust are required to drop out.

Accounting figures prominently in the curriculum, too. No one gets past that class until he or she knows the cost-per-nail-per-day to hang a painting, what is fifty percent of a dollar, how to make change and handle charges on Visa and Mastercard or Discover.

No session is complete without students digesting techniques to deal sympathetically with artists. Applicants are required to use phrases which build confidence in aspiring artists while pointing them toward the door. Favorites are: *"Shows real promise. Keep at it. Keep in touch. Not in our market, but I'm keeping you in mind."*

Former Ad Execs Make Best Salespeople

As potential gallery owners, they are cautioned against ever employing art school graduates. The brains of these individuals are overfilled with art idiom and they may tend to overwhelm customers with information. The best salespeople to hire, according to the school, are former advertising executives who have the moral principles of chipmunks and will sell anything.

One of the most important classes before graduation is learning *collector-speak*. This requires extensive reading and digesting of articles in *Art Muse* and *Art in Antarctica*. The final examination includes at least two obscure articles appearing in those magazines which must be correctly interpreted to complete the course. This is perhaps the most difficult assignment because writers in these magazines limit themselves to no more than one period per paragraph plus a tiny sprinkling of commas.

In addition, they have created a whole new language fashioned from old, previously common words. These must now be divined as the applicant reads the articles and hopes for the best interpretation.

A short example which seemed to give one student a small problem in deciphering was:

"The concept seemed to self-generate from the elegiac atmosphere of the gergen to an ironic confabulation situated between pastiche and dialecticism. It is a reincarnation of the Amphitryon ideal, crossing the subtle line between allegorical sentences and didactic constructionism."

The crowning achievement for those who "make it," is the opportunity to join the ranks of the few and proud who wear the GOLD PICTURE-HANGER RING. It announces to the world and each comrade-in-art that the wearer is a member of "the exclusive in-club" of trained and responsible gallery owners and managers.

The much-prized ring is awarded by the NYAGTI president and faculty in an emotional ceremony marked by solemnity, good friends and elegant refreshments. The event is usually packed with artists who will attend anything which offers free food. Family members of the prospective gallery owners are often tearful during graduation, for I have heard more than one mother sob, "As long as he is graduating, so why can't he graduate a doctor or a lawyer or maybe even a dentist and *make something of himself?*"

Some Parents Eventually Come To Terms With Chosen Career

In time, these parents and relatives come to accept and even in some cases, to encourage their offspring in their chosen profession of selling art and talking a second language.

Thus, graduation is simply a short step on the road to successful gallery management for these highly trained, ambitious women and men.

When you visit a gallery and see the famed Gold Picture Hanger Ring adorning the pinkie of the owner or manager, remember this: You are in the presence of one of the few, the proud and the professional guardians of our art marketplace.

Paid Advertisements

Chapter 10

News of the World,
As reported by the *Sturbill Free Press:*

Second Paint-By-Number International Awards Dinner Draws Huge Throng

Over 833 people attended the second International Paint-by-Number Juried Competition, Convention, and Dinner Dance held last week in the beautiful Freon Room of the Gerblatzen Hotel.

"The turnout was outstanding," claimed Ms. H.C. Schlogdrip, awards-juror. She is the author of *Why You Don't Have To Know Much About Art To Know What You Don't Like.*

Forty-five prizes were handed out to the international contestants that evening.

Tells Paint-By-Number History

Keynote speaker was the Vice President of the United States. She was roundly cheered for her inspiring welcoming speech, which included some little-known history of the ancient paint-by-number process. "It started with the Egyptians," she explained, " because the Egyptians knew, just as we have learned, that keeping within established and universal lines of understanding is to maintain our traditional family values."

Paint by
numbers
AWARDS

She concluded her keynote address with a special request to sing and play on her bass drum, "I've Got Your Number." The audience gave her a standing ovation.

Schwarzenegger Demonstrates

Master of ceremonies, Arnold Schwarzenegger, received a standing ovation for his demonstration painting, "Red Rose in Blue Vase" (Norton Pattern No. 325). Holding his hands up to the audience, he quipped, "Even vit dese big muscle-fingers, I can do dis delicate verk."

The British Consul to Oslo, Windon B.C.F. Dripwerth, OBE, LBJ, CBE, accepted the silver prize for the entry of England's Prince Charles. Mr. Schwarzenegger apologized for the title misprint in the program which read "Danielle's Panties." It should have read "Danielle's Pansies."

Youngest Winner Only 24-Months Old

The prize for the youngest contestant went to Imogene Dwebble. Although Imogene is only

24-months old and just learning her numbers, she finished her painting without any outside help, her mother and father announced as they accepted Imogene's prize. This was greeted by deafening applause and cheering from the audience. Imogene was unable to accept her award personally because her father, Grimaldi Dwebble, affectionately told the crowd that it was past her bedtime.

There was a moment of silence when the prize for the oldest contestant for her painting, "Mirror Mountain," was awarded posthumously to Eldren Binkensorken of Green Meadows Nursing Home, Green Meadows, Ohio. Had she lived, Eldren would have been somewhere between 111 and 115.

"Horse" Dorfer Wins Grand Prize

Heinz (Horse) Dorfer of Dortmund, Germany, won the Grand Prize for "Seurat's Sunday in the Park," which, painted in the "pointillist" style, included over 14000 spaces and required a 40-foot ladder and seven years to complete. For his acceptance speech, Mr. Dorfer simply exclaimed, "I would never do THAT again! Not by a long shot!"

A Special Prize was awarded to Emilio Subriana by the King of Norway, for his "Mother Love" (Gorbley Pattern 11C) on black velvet. When completed, it resembled a pillow.

Following musical numbers by Kathleen Battle and Luciano Pavarotti, the convention was adjourned and the celebrants returned to their hotels and homes. Many said they were gleefully looking forward to the challenge of the new paintings they will be undertaking. A large number say they will keep their fingers crossed in hope to be included in the even greater gala scheduled next year in Prague.

Paid Advertisements

105

"That's the showpiece of my studio!"

Earn An <u>Artistic</u> <u>License</u> In Your Spare Time At Home!

Doesn't it give you a feeling of comfort to visit your doctor and see his doctor's licenses hanging on the wall? Just seeing that piece of parchment with the little ribbons stuck to that cute embossed foil thing somehow makes us think we're in the right place at the right time.

How often have you shivered in your altogether and been impressed by credentials from all those universities and hospitals? Yes, where would doctors be without licenses? Lawyers and dentists and accountants have them, too.

You can bet big bucks that Pablo Picasso, Mondrian, Matisse, Kandinsky, Pollock, Marin and Rothko all had Artistic Licenses.

Same for Motherwell, Raphael, Frank Stella, Luca Della Robbia, Andrew Wyeth, Roy Litchenstein, Roy Rodgers, Jasper Johns, Burt Silverman, Bronzini, Bellini, Bonfigli, Bonifazio, Bonnard -- all the artists whose names begin with B, plus Alex Powers, Tom Sgouros and Milt Kobayashi.

Why shouldn't you also have one and make your wall equally impressive?

Now you can do something about it. Let us send you our qualifying questionnaire free of charge. Study the questions for at least ten minutes before you put down your answers. Don't worry. The questions aren't hard and we've never turned down an applicant. When you return the completed form to us along with $69.95 to cover International Registration, postage and handling, we will mail you YOUR ARTISTIC LICENSE with THE SEAL OF THE ACADEMY and your name PRINTED BOLDLY as the honoree.

Watch Your Paintings Go Up in Value Practically Overnight!

Think of the confidence you'll inspire in visitors to your studio when they see this framed document on your wall! Think how much more your paintings will be worth! But don't wait. THIS OFFER IS LIMITED to anyone who writes:

International Global Artistic Academy

Pearl D. V. Oyster, FHA, PHD, President
American Licensing Division
Box 7, Grapeshot IN 75003

Paid Advertisements

Chapter 11

Sven Svenderen AUS, UPS
Reports a True-Life Experience in:

An Unusual Workshop with Ardeth

Recently I attended a unique
workshop conducted by a 637-pound female

Ardeth works furiously as we watch!

gorilla named Ardeth. I know it seems highly unusual, but let me tell you a fascinating success story.

About three years ago, Ardeth was being trained in speech by Ms. Candace Neal at the gorilla laboratory connected to the University of Rhode Island. Ardeth's job was to press a red button if she understood the word or phrase her trainer used, a blue button if she was unsure and a yellow button if she wanted to be excused to go to the restroom. Her performance was excellent and she had amassed a vocabulary of over 800 words, about 300 more than today's average high school graduate.

Ardeth Learns About Abstract Art

One day, to give herself some time off, her trainer handed Ardeth some paints and a book on abstract art which she had picked up in one of the classrooms. When Ms. Neal returned to the laboratory after taking her pleasure with Dr. Zerbel Frasco, she was shocked to see the painting Ardeth had executed.

At first she couldn't believe her eyes. She had had an art class and was amazed that the work went beyond deKooning in design concept and rivaled Joan Mitchell in color creativity. Ms. Neal looked at Ardeth who was just finishing the last pages of the book. When she finished jotting down a few notes for reference, Ardeth looked up and signaled she was ready for another canvas.

In just a matter of two weeks, Ardeth finished an amazing body of work. Twenty-five pieces in all. At that point, Ms. Neal thought no one would believe these paintings could have been executed by a gorilla, and decided to show them to a major New York gallery, claim them as her own, and cleverly pocket the proceeds.

Ardeth Gets Glowing Revues

Needless to say, the gallery owner was stunned, even overwhelmed by the work supposedly created by this young woman, and immediately scheduled a major one-person show. Critics hailed the arrival of a new art genius in glowing revues in the New York Times and all major art magazines. The event was a sellout!

Meanwhile, back in Rhode Island, Dr. Fasco was facing a probable divorce suit at the hands of a furious, jealous wife. To demonstrate loyalty to his spouse, he denounced Neal as an art fraud with an unhealthy sexual appetite. The resulting uncovering of Ms. Neal's scheme made national TV. Furious collectors returned their paintings to the gallery, crying they weren't paying top dollar for work done by wild "baboons" [sic].

Ms. Neal was sentenced to a prison term of two years, taught language arts to other inmates and was released for good behavior three months later. She subsequently changed her name and is thought to be employed by a zoo in Australia.

Dr. Fasco remained married but temporarily unemployed. He continues to undergo a long-term program of treatment with a therapist named Sally.

Ardeth Find Her Place Teaching Painting Workshops

As to Ardeth, she found herself with time on her hands, a unique artistic talent without a market and the ability to understand 800 words. What to do with her life? After some months in therapy with a Dr. Kline, she decided she had both the talent and necessary vocabulary to teach painting workshops. When I saw her listing in American Artist and Artists' magazine, I signed up for a five-day session in Kansas City and that's where we met and I began to learn the full story.

We Start With Very Grueling Physical Training

Classes were held in the basement of a local church, where we set up our easels first thing Monday morning. It amazed all of us, her students, that within minutes we could fully comprehend Ardeth's language of soft or loud grunts and howls and know exactly how we were to proceed.

We started the first morning with a healthy meal of two to three bananas. This was our breakfast throughout the five-day workshop. Then came the physical training. Here we learned to assume the simian posture, imitating Ardeth as we followed her around the room during her demonstration. This was vital, Ardeth told us, as she felt her strength came from lurching around on all fours. Until we became used to it, it seemed very tiring to walk around the room with our hands scraping the floor. But by Wednesday, we had pretty well mastered it, and had even learned to grunt with subtle modulations so we could communicate with Ardeth on a primitive but very meaningful level.

We Work With Our Hands!

The painting technique was an eye-opener. After Ardeth showed us how she painted, we went to work. We learned to paint entirely without knife or brushes, simply dipping both our hands into the colors and applying them to the canvas in a furious, rhythmic application as Ardeth demonstrated. The natural structures, the movement, the colors, the pure wildness of it! It truly was the most exciting workshop I ever attended and I think I can speak for the entire class when I say that.

Ardeth would walk among us and watch us paint. She would make encouraging little grunts and when we did something she really liked, she would pat us on our backs. But with all those 637 pounds behind her she would often knock us off our feet, but we would usually laugh as we tried to get up. I still remember Mary Elizabeth Wonk taking one such tap and flying out a window. Now that I recall, I don't remember her ever returning to her easel.

Although I finished that class only two years ago, my new work is now showing in three of the most prestigious galleries in New York and Paris and earning critical reviews. Sales are in seven figures.

I will never forget Ardeth's contribution to my career. To this day, I start each day with my lurching exercises and eat at least three bananas. I also seem to be growing more facial hair and that embarrassing bald spot I tried to hide is now completely covered with a thick new growth.

I never fail to recommend her classes to other artists and try to keep in touch by phoning or sending her a card each Christmas and on her birthday.

Paid Advertisements

To Ethel, Box BVD: I couldn't help noticing your classified ad in which you would like to donate the paintings of C.J. Lemming to a worthy museum for a permanent collection. Am I to understand Mr. Lemming painted watercolors of Camp Wicheehwheree? Did you also say he did a painting of your daughter at her first tap-dancing class? These are EXACTLY the type of paintings the Fungus Museum of Art has been searching for throughout the world to include in our permanent collection. What a momentous coincidence! I only hope I am in time for you to consider the considerable facilities of the Fungus. I am sure I will be in your area within the next few hours, and would love to drop by for a visit to discuss the magnificent contribution these Lemming watercolors will make to the Fungus, America and the Art World. Fax me, **Dudley Fempster Sploggle III, Director, Fungus Museum, Box PH.**

Editor's Note:
We regret we could not include more than one of the hundreds of responses by Art Museum directors throughout the U.S. to the wonderful, generous letter of Mrs. Ethel Lemming. We are personally heartened by the overwhelming enthusiasm of the many museum directors to include C. J. Lemming's watercolors in their permanent collections. They all seemed to feel that the painting by Mr. Lemming of his daughter at her first tap-dancing class was a much-prized work even though they hadn't seen it. Again, we are sorry that lack of space prevents us from including these many letters, but we have passed all of them on to Mrs. Lemming.

Have You Tried Your Hand at Forgery? Law enforcement officers are looking full-time for drug dealers. That leaves big opportunities for forgers to REALLY MAKE BIG MONEY unmolested. If you like to copy things, particularly pictures of Presidents and famous American Statesmen and love the color green, then this may be your big break. Call Harry the Horse from a phone booth, but don't tell anybody! Just stand there and pretend you didn't see this ad. I'LL CONTACT YOU!

Create More Meaningful Art by Learning the Meaning of Life.
The secret has been revealed to Pazwal Sturdily, through OSMOTIC REFLUGATION. He will share the message. Request "Fountain Circular." Send no money now. Write **Pazwal, Box WOW.**

Madame ZsuZsu gets answers first-hand.

Chapter 12

Ask the Art Expert

Have a question about art?
Madame ZsuZsu KNOWS ALL!

Dear Madam ZsuZsu: Did Francis Bacon, who wrote everything under the name of Shakespeare, still have time to do all of the paintings ascribed to Rembrandt?

Joe X Bushman, Shedrain, New York

Answer: You're right! Francis Bacon was a talented writer and painter who never used his real name for his art or plays. As a child he was constantly teased and called "Hambone" or "Piggy" or "Pigface" or "Francis" until he was reduced to tears. We don't know how he came up with the name *Shakespeare*, but we now know he chose *Rembrandt* because he saw it on a tube of paint and said it sounded nice.

* * * * *

Dear Zsu Zsu: We know that Winsor and Newton were the first to put paint in lead tubes, but who was first to discover how to get the lead out?

Bushman X Joel, Shedrain, New York

Answer: Don't joke with me. This is a serious column.

* * * * *

Dear ZsuZsu: What was the name of the first artist to discover if you mixed red and green, you got yellow. Or was it yellow and green and you got red? Anyway, who?

Elmer Sturdily, Spokane, Washington

Answer: I don't remember his name, but if he got the mixes you describe, you both must be color blind. Red and green do not make yellow. They make a kind of a blue.

* * * * *

Dear ZsuZsu: I always wondered what was Whistler's mother telling him while he painted her in "Arrangement in Black and Gray"?

D. Carnegie, Memphis, Nova Scotia

Answer: To find out, we searched through Whistler's Diary (featured in his 1884 painting, "Arrangement in Red and White on Table) and found these quotations:

"Don't whistle while you paint. It's very annoying. I hope you don't make me all gray and black like you usually do. Did you remember to get your teeth cleaned? Where did you leave my

book of poems that nice Mr. Standish gave me?
You know the Stephensons are coming tonight for
dinner? Don't be late. I certainly hope you're
not going to take out that Molly Anderson. She
really is not our sort. Where do you go these
days? You're never home. Did you remember to
take out the garbage? How late did you get in last
night? I was up 'til after midnight. I had so much
on my mind and I didn't hear you come in. Your
friends drink too much and you're beginning to
drink too much, too. I really don't like those men
you hang around with. I worry so much about
you...

* * * * *

Dear ZsuZsu: What did Whistler say in reply?
Sven Svendersen, Bjorkland, Ontario

Answer: Mumble...mumble...mumble

* * * * *

Dear ZsuZsu: Who was the first woman artist
who married an alien being straight off the
starship Schlep and taught art to the Gynos on the
Planet Plotrec II in Craftick B constellation?
Clifton Fabulous, Greenville SC

Answer: Irma Greenbaum of Strudel, Minnesota. Her husband says he has not seen or heard from her although she said she would keep in touch with him and their 11 children. Mr. Greenbaum has purchased a Bushnell Super XXL Telescope and looks heavenward every night for a sign. (*See National Inquirer, Aug. 12, 1943.*)

* * * * *

Dear ZsuZsu: Who was the first artist who accidentally knocked over a can of black paint on a half completed canvas in 1938 and didn't have enough sense to show it in New York and become rich and famous?

Ferd Friendly, Sarasota, New Mexico

Answer: Smalmar Hilderfrtuz of Shelbyville, Tennessee, who was known to the local residents as just plain "Slob." He died penniless and without friends. His last 30 paintings are still hanging in the Mobilgas station on Main and Thromboid.

* * * * *

Dear ZsuZsu: I notice that Bruegel The Elder in "The Peasant Wedding," painted three legs on the man in red carrying the board filled with pies or something. Did Bruegel just make a mistake or what?

Eliza Doolittle, Hartford-Herefordshire, England

Answer: No, Bruegel was faithful to the facts. The model had three legs and was an odds-on favorite to win every three-legged race in the region and raced without need of a partner.

* * * * *

Dear ZsuZsu: I am confused by Monet and Manet, the impressionist(s). Were they the same person with poor handwriting, or were they two people and related?

Sylvia Banff, Banfff, Hungary

Answer: I can't tell you how many letters I get every year with this question! Monet and Manet actually were brothers. As immigrants, they came to Ellis Island separately, and immigration officials, not adept at foreign pronunciations, misspelled their name twice. It should have been

spelled <u>Manney</u> in English. The young men,
fearful of breaking the laws of their newly adopted
land, never had their names changed legally.

* * * * *

Dear ZsuZsu: Why is the Museum Of Modern
Art in New York sometimes referred to as
MOMA?

Archimedes Antikythera, Athens, GA

Answer: MOMA stands for Mother of Mucho
(great or big) Art because it houses one of the
largest collections in the world. Sort of like
Mother Of All Battles, or Mother Of All Mothers,
or Mother of...You get the general idea.

* * * * *

Dear ZsuZsu: Why did the ancient Egyptians
paint people with only one eye? I mean the
paintings had one eye. Not the painters, as far as I
know..

Ulysses Sload Grant, Grubber KA

Answer: Eyes are hard to paint and if the artist
got one right that was good enough. Hands and

feet are also hard to paint and should be left out of all paintings if possible.

****

Dear ZsuZsu: I am a beginner and my uncle would like to have me do a painting of the beach. What color do I use for sand?

Little Imogene Sulfur, Salem OR

Answer: You are in luck, little lady! Winsor & Newton has just introduced four new colors in their oil and watercolor painting line which are exactly what you need. They are "Wet sand," "Dry Sand," "Wet Rocks," and "Dry Rocks". Simply pick up a few small tubes and use them as needed.

****

Want the answer?

If you have always wondered about some perplexing question relating to art and would like the answer, but you couldn't ask anyone before because you were afraid word would go out that you were stupid, write Madame ZsuZsu, Box A, Salem, WE 66626.

For submitting a best question *you may win a free dried-up paint brush actually used by* Madame ZsuZsu *in one of her fine oil and sand paintings of* Sunsets Behind Debble Mountain.

Paid Advertisements

Learn Gallery Management : One or two week courses teach you everything you need to know about running a successful art gallery. Learn how to identify stone, copper and other sculpting materials, watercolors, oils. How to talk to customers, how to separate artists from buyers, how to make change, how to tell non-customers you don't have public restrooms. Classes held late July, early August when New York is at its prettiest. Write: **New York Art Gallery Training Institute, Box NY.**

Joan : I simply can't live without you. I know I may do something desperate if you don't come back and I don't want you to feel the tremendous guilt if anything should happen to me. Please reconsider and come back. The frozen dinners are all gone and we don't have many pages to write each other left in this book! **Paul, Box ABC.**

Older Artist : Wants to get out of rat race. Successful career painting and selling LIGHT PASSING THROUGH CRASHING WAVES OVER ROCKS TYPE SCENES. Making life-change and moving to Midwest to take over Mother's barber shop. Will sell entire lot of art supplies dirt cheap. Many tubes of paint, some still with caps, lots of almost clean brushes, palettes, canvasses, painty rags, nude model, stool, the works. First offer takes all. **Ralph, Box VV.**

Train to be an art juror! More jurors in greater demand for art exhibitions around US. Great opportunities, big money. Learn to reject bad art, okay good work, award prizes, be looked up to, fawned over, treated with respect. Travel, enjoy good food, accommodations all free to you. No art experience necessary. We train you. Our school has had over 20 years experience training baseball and basketball umpires. We know how to give you the expertise to make decisions even in the face of bodily harm. For prospectus, write **Global Institute, Box ZX.**

New Miracle Brush! Tried everything, but nothing works for long? Even $5000 Kolinsky Sables? New miracle brush keeps point electrically. Tiny batteries (not included) in handle automatically straighten bristles at night while U sleep. CR says, "Fabulous!" BL calls it best brush she ever used! Write for prices, sizes. Money-back guarantee. **Electrobrush, Box GG.**

130

Famous artists are waiting for your call!

course it may be too late for some of them, but think of what you can learn speaking to TODAY'S FAMOUS ARTISTS. Artists you've read about, whose work you love and admire!

They're Waiting By Their Phones!

Just dial the number below, ask for the artists you want and START TALKING. Tell them about problems you're having with a work you're creating and ask for their advice. Maybe you need a change of direction and they can give you some answers. Ask what galleries they might recommend to represent you. Perhaps they could even put in a good word for you to get you into a prestigious gallery!

Call several times so you really get to know them. Be sure to ask after their families and tell them about *your* loved ones. Talk about your personal problems and find out if they can offer constructive suggestions. Famous people also have emotional hangups and they may want to discuss them with *you, too*!

Ask them how they're doing! Tell them what you're up to. Name names, talk about shows, gallery owners, what's new with you. Ask personal questions. Share funny stories. Even discuss colors they use, brands they prefer, stuff about brushes, color mixing, lots of things like that.

Maybe make arrangements to stay overnight or for the weekend or just get together sometime for lunch or even a movie or perhaps a family picnic!

What opportunities for budding artists to learn from their idols! Ideal gift for your nieces, nephews, grandparents or other relatives who show creative talent and would like to hear a real artist's voice or maybe would just like to know how long it takes for them to do a painting. Just get your phone handy. They're waiting for your call NOW!

Look! These Are Just A Few Of The Artists On Our Extensive List You Can Call:

Frank Stella
Alex Powers
Joan Ashley Rothermel
Larry Rivers
Andrew Wyeth

The Wyeth Family of Artists (a conference call,
    $2.55 minute extra)
Fred Wong
Jean Dobie
Don Andrews
Gerald Brommer
Dong Kingman
Roy Litchenstein
Jasper Johns
Burt Silverman
Tom Sgouros
Milt Kobayashi
Wayne Thiebaud

Plus Many More in Our Extensive Free Catalog!

Talk to Dead Artists, Too!

Famous Artcalls *can offer you messages digitally recorded and programmed to respond to your questions like a real live conversation! These inspirational words were captured on tape just before they died. Converse with Pablo Picasso, Eakins, Berthe Morrisot, Giacometti, Michelangelo, Chagall, Rodin, Cassat, Renoir,*

DaVinci, Raphael, Motherwell, Seurat, Vermeer, Rousseau, and many other dead favorites! Take your pick and be thrilled!

Do You Have Your Phone Handy?
Dial right now:

Famous Artcalls

29 Victoria Gardens, Burnside, Utah 80123

CALL 1-900-ART-0000

follow instructions and say
"VISA OR MASTERCARD,"
then your number,
and just start talking!

Paid Advertisements

Paul : I have had a very bad shock and can hardly breathe! I guess I misjudged your strength, your goodness and your faithfulness. I found out why Dashiel, that pig, had to be away at "work" so much of the time. He had a wife and children and was just using me! I was simply devastated when his wife, Serva, came with Dashiel's eleven children to my little temporary studio. They are darling and they all got on their knees --all eleven of them -- and pleaded with me to lay off their dad. What could I do but submit to their entreaties and cry uncontrollably. Then, my tears dripped onto a painting of agapanthas I had been working on for days and ruined it! Well, that's it! I now know I've been fooling myself. I really missed you and the children more than I could have imagined. I will take the first flight home and call you from the airport. **Joan, Box LOVE.**

"Gor. Did I just feel the tail twitch?
Or was that my imagination?

Chapter 13

The origin of the paint-brush

Simple as it appears, our modern

paintbrush is a tribute to man's ingenuity. Or more

accurately, man's bumping into things by accident. Like falling into wet dirt and discovering MUD. Know what I mean?

Twelve eons ago, two major developments contributing to our present-day brush were taking place concurrently in the West and East. In the West, ancient man discovered the stick, which he used to kill animals and scratch patterns into soft clay. Although it worked OK for some things, a few complained that it was hard to spread paint with a stick. During a regular weekly business meeting of the clan, the chief witch doctor explained, "Stick-painting is demanded by the gods. That's what makes us superior to animals."

Explanation Makes Sense

That explanation so satisfied the artists that they picked up their sticks and went back to work.

Meanwhile, on the other side of the world, there lived the sable people.

These Cro-Magnets originally painted with the tails of sleeping saber-toothed tigers, but the mortality rate was so high among artists that smaller furry animals were, of necessity, tested.

As luck would have it, on Thursday they discovered Kolinsky Sables, which had evolved that day, opening their little beady eyes just around noon.

Imagine the shock and bewilderment! Those little sables just waking up after eons of really strenuous evolution and some ugly hair-covered goon is grabbing them by the neck! How traumatic for the little rascals to yawn and stretch and scratch for the first time and find themselves already on the endangered species list!

Sables Have Drawback

Well, anyway, those Cro-Magnet ape creature artists would spread paint on those cute cuddly sables which they held in their hands. Then they would rub their little backs on flat pieces of rock to create crude paintings. As you can imagine, delicate work was almost impossible to achieve without paws. The primary drawback to this painting technique was that the little critters would bite the hand that guided it, as well as other parts, if their fur was rubbed the wrong way.

About two-and-a-quarter eons ago, during the Flem period, Stefano, one of the stick people, created havoc among the tribe. He was caught THINKING -- which still wasn't approved yet. Forced to flee for his life with his favorite stick, he eventually settled on the other side of the world, among the sable people. When he saw what pains these people were taking with their paintings (getting bitten, maimed and chewed to death), he made a suggestion:

"Why not tie a stick to the little sables?" he asked, adding, "You will have greater control and less bleeding."

Since thinking hadn't yet appeared among these people either, it caused a violent outcry and the elders pushed him in front of the first Brontosaurus cruising through. Although his idea was never adopted, it was added to the oral history of the people. The recitation of that portion in the communal celebrations was always greeted with derisive laughter and obscene gestures.

Barbie and Ken Make Appearance

One day, as chance would have it, a pair of Republozoic craftsmen named Barbie and Ken, who had heard this story since childhood but were confused about the technique, simply tied some of the FUR instead of the WHOLE ANIMAL to a stick. Before they could correct their error, they laid a brushload of paint on a stone and lo and behold, Oriental calligraphy and modern painting were born!

Thus evolved the fundamental tool we can't be without today, even though one thing has dramatically changed. The stick is the same, but now much of the sable has been replaced by a type of fur made from pigs, goats, moles, squirrels, slugs, and oil-fed, hairy animals evidently made of plastic.

Paid Advertisement

Homer Gerbil finds his personal art niche.

Chapter 14

Nicheing (pronounced "nitching")

Or how to reach your place in the sun as an artist

Artists are notorious for envying the styles of other painters, living and dead. Ask almost any artist how he likes his work and he'll tell you he wished he could paint like someone else.

So there you have it. Never content, most artists constantly grope for a satisfying niche -- a place in the sun -- which simply eludes them. And that also goes for artists of yesteryear, too.

Rejected by Franklin Mint

Renoir would have ended up unhappily painting pretty china cups and saucers all his life if he had not been rejected by both the Franklin and Danbury Mints. They didn't think his stuff had enough mass appeal to sell in large circulation publications like *Parade* magazine. But that rejection was the lucky stroke which led him to discover his niche: to mass produce paintings of the same pretty girl in a variety of poses, adding other people and children as needed. The public loved the work and he became *The Impressionist Of Choice* at the Metropolitan Museum of Art.

What about Michelangelo? Lying on his back for five years painting the ceiling of the Sistine Chapel and visiting his chiropractor every other day convinced him that he had to find a new niche. It came to him one day when he stood up and stretched!

"Why not WORK VERTICALLY!" he asked himself. He did and became a legend. Isn't that a heartwarming story?

Larry Rivers always had trouble painting bodies. Faces came OK but he kept smudging out bodies, trying again and again to get them right. Paint, smudge, paint, smudge. Finally he found the niche he was looking for and became a successful artist. He just left the smudges on the canvas and the public thought he was a genius.

Pollock Gives Up Realistic Figurative Work

Jackson Pollock was forced by a case of nerves to abandon brushes in favor of dribbling paint. A shaky hand interfered with his realistic figurative work and one day he accidentally dropped a can of paint on a canvas he had left on the floor. When he stopped swearing himself blue in the face, he realized he had found his niche and became the father of "action painting."

Many artists are faced with similar dilemmas. They have been painting in a certain

147

style and feel they must make a change. But what change? Should they paint horses, or landscapes, or abstracts or blank canvases or imitate other artists? What? In short, they are looking for a niche.

There Is A Niche For You!

If you're one of many who haven't found that "right" approach to your art yet, you are in luck. Now you can stop wasting valuable art time, forever looking and looking, because The Niche Society of America can offer you a choice from over 112 unique niches they have catalogued and computerized.

Imagine the joy of having YOUR VERY OWN NICHE from *PLEXIGLAS BLOWING* to *ABSTRACT ENCOUNTER PAINTING OF THE THIRD KIND ON BLACK VELVET.* This is indeed a wonderful opportunity to find yourself and be famous and envied!

Simply write The Society, Box 8, Umpteen Station, New York. Tell them about your present unfortunate niche, a description of your terrible childhood, something about how much you were teased at school because you were "different", and

$400. That will entitle you to choose your personal niche and a fallback one if the first one doesn't work out (literally two niches for the price of one). We are informed that the Society will then mail you your tastefully engraved certificate announcing your new niche with your very own name applied in hand-done calligraphy. This is nicely framed and suitable for hanging on a studio or home wall next to your Artistic License. It will announce to one and all that you have finally found yourself.

The Society informs us that if you order now, they will also mail you a set of steak knives which sharpen themselves at night while you sleep.

Paid Advertisements

Chapter 15

Sandscor Dingbat, Underwater Painter

Fourteen years ago when Sandscor Dingbat was passing through a gallery in

"Sandy! Hurry it up. This fish
is beginning to stink!"

San Francisco, he happened to stop and look at a tiny painting in a very large mat and frame. It was a painting of a single cherry and it was priced at $3000. A painter himself, Sandscor naturally stuck his nose right up to the glass to see how the artist had done it.

A voice behind him said, "That's very difficult to do."

Sandscor turned to see a pretty young woman.

"The reason that's priced the way it is, is because it is very difficult to do," she repeated. Then she went on to explain for about 15 minutes, how long it takes to craft a cherry the way the artist did, the tools used, the knives, stones, block and tackle, tractor, trial and error, the painstaking technique, etc. There was a lot of etc. Sandscor was enthralled.

He had always wanted to sell his paintings for high prices, but didn't know the secret to becoming rich and famous. Now he knew. A painting had to be difficult and take a long time to do. He repeated the phrase to himself many times so he wouldn't forget it as he walked to his car, sometimes saying it out loud. Passersby moved out of his way.

"The Skydiving Painter!"

When he reached his Pontiac, he started her up and drove all the way home to Utah. Just driving and thinking and it hit him. "The skydiving painter!" He would take up skydiving, learn to do it well, then paint as he free-fell. It would be time-consuming, too, because he had only seconds to paint during each dive and it would take many dives to complete a painting. Difficult and time-consuming! It had all the ingredients.

As soon as he could check the Yellow Pages for skydiving schools and make an appointment, he was on his way. While the instructor explained the procedure on the ground, Sandscor repeatedly interrupted, "Can't we get a move on? I AM in a hurry!"

Realizes Fear of Heights

He was then fitted with a parachute, hastened aboard the plane, and when it reached the correct altitude, the instructor signaled to Sandscor, "Jump!" Sandscor froze. "Take me down," he said. "Now I realize why I didn't do this before. I'm afraid of heights."

Decides To Paint Underwater

When safely back on the ground and in his car heading home, Sandscor snapped his fingers, and laughed to himself, "I'm afraid of heights, but not afraid of depths, and if it's going to be diving, it's me for the water. I will be the first and only underwater painter! Difficult and time-consuming. Yeah!"

First thing Sandscor did was to build a special swimming tank in his studio. It was 6 feet by 6 feet by 10 feet deep (to add depth to his paintings.) It had heavy glass sides so he could look out to see what he wanted to paint. The pool company thought it was stupid, but Sandscor fitted it with toys he thought appropriate and set to work filling it. He could hardly wait to dive in.

New Method Requires Non-Floating Supplies

Next, Sandscor outfitted himself with everything he would need. Waterproof watercolors and oil paints, special lead brushes that wouldn't float, an aluminum palette, a stainless steel easel, a heavy lead weight tied to an ankle so he could secure himself on the floor of the pool while painting.

Eschews Air Tank (He didn't use one.)

He considered an air tank but dismissed the idea because if he could stay down for hours at a time, he could finish a painting too quickly. "Time-consuming, it has to be time-consuming," he said to himself. "I'll just take deep breaths, dive in and paint, then come up for air frequently," he said to himself.

His first painting took over a year with only one weekend off, and required 4,012 dives to complete. Painted *plein H2O*, it pictured a large can of tuna and it was titled simply, "Tuna in Can." The first gallery owner in San Francisco who saw it literally jumped out of her black patent pumps. "How did you do this?" she asked.

"It was very difficult and time-consuming," Sandscor replied. Then he explained the process for 15 minutes while the proprietor's jaw locked open. When he had finished, the gallery owner in ecstasy, hugged Sandscor.

"It is the magic formula!" she wept. "We'll price it at $5,000. And I will need 25 more for the show I'm already planning! It will be a sensation! Run home and get started!"

25 Years is a Long Time for a Painting!

As he was driving slowly back to Utah, Sandscor thought to himself, "25 more. WOW! 25 more. *Hmm.* 25 more years. 25 MORE YEARS!" He turned the car around, returned to the gallery, grabbed the painting before the owner could object and sped back to Utah.

That magic painting now hangs on his wall at home. If you see him selling at the mall, ask if you might see that painting. The pool has been dismantled and Sandscor has returned to painting swift watercolors of Bryce Canyon and Orem.

"Fast and furious! That's my motto now," he tells friends. "Heck," he says, "my prices may be low but I can make that up in the large quantity I can paint. Besides, I never realized how much I enjoyed breathing regularly."

Paid Advertisements

Chapter 16

Miramar Kline, Artist Therapist

famous troubled artists
a specialty

The silence made me squirm a little. I had been ushered into the office of Dr. Kline,

Soo...You say you cannot get those numbers out of your mind?

the psychoanalyst who specialized in working with the problems of artists, particularly famous ones. She peered at me over her half-glasses.

I had been directed to sit on the gray leather couch, still warm from a previous artist's bottom. She took a chair facing me, crossed her legs and looked at me. Her Mont Blanc pen was poised to make notes on the yellow legal pad on her lap. "Yes?" she asked.

I Confess to Trouble With Lines

I fidgeted a bit, then said quietly, "I have difficulty when I encounter lines."

"You have trouble with lines?" she repeated as she rose, set the alarm clock behind my head and softly returned to her chair.

"Yes," I said.

There was a heavy silence. Neither of us spoke.

Finally she said, "This is nothing to be ashamed of."

I responded by telling her that she shouldn't end a sentence with a preposition.

She thanked me, made a note, then looked up at me with some new-found respect, I felt, and we went on.

"I don't seem to have the courage to paint past lines. I always end a given color at the line and I know I should disregard the lines at times to gain some nice "lost edges" but I have these fears," I whispered. "I think I blame my teachers and society for this terrible failing and lack of control," I added.

After a pregnant silence, she glanced at the clock and said, "Continue."

I told her about my childhood, how I was forced to take up drinking, smoking, and sex by friends who led me astray, how we were too poor to afford a grand piano, how I loved to eat crayons until I was blue in the face, how I was beaten by teachers, my loves, my hates, my fears, my God.

I had only covered three years before she glanced again at the little clock behind my head and informed me that my 45 minutes were up. I begged for another 5 minutes to cover at least six more months, but she ignored my entreaty. As I was putting on my coat, the alarm went off.

Since our first meeting, we have met together 52 times and I have resolved many of my problems and now can actually ERASE some lines and disregard others. It has been a real breakthrough in my painting.

Most important, I have learned a great deal more about how Dr. Kline has helped others.

Dr. Kline Helps Realist Painters

For instance, she has worked with a number of famous painters whose names she, of course, cannot reveal. But they have one problem in common. They are realist painters who are either given nasty reviews or who are regularly ignored, even reviled, by critics writing in Art Muse, Art in Antarctica or daily newspapers and magazines.

She deals with their pain, which never goes away. Many have been her patients for over ten years. And they still get bad or no reviews but now they drive Ferraris and Mercedes and own large homes with swimming pools and belong to exclusive clubs and feel they can handle the pain better.

She tells me she usually gets a large influx of patients who have been rejected by juried shows. In fact, she can count on at least a dozen or more new watercolor-artist patients calling for therapy right after the American Watercolor Society and the Allied Artists or other major shows return their unaccepted slides.

"It usually takes several visits before they feel good about themselves again, but it can be done," she said.

"The most important thing is to deal with it, and not simply go to a movie or hurt others in anger, or ignore it," she added. "Failure is part of life."

I reached over and lightly touched her arm. I had also experienced failure and her words were profoundly meaningful to me.

Gallery Owners Refer To Her Card For Emergency Cases

"I also get other artist patients. Some ask for appointments when galleries they have approached are uninterested in carrying their work. In fact, it is not unusual for gallery owners to call and tell me to expect rings from certain artists they have passed over," she added. "Almost all our gallery owners and managers keep one of my cards in an emergency file."

"I also have gallery owners among my patients. Some of them are experiencing particularly painful frustration dealing well with non-buying customers they refer to as *tire kickers*. I try to help them deal with the deep hurt they feel when people walk out of their galleries without buying something. It's particularly hard, and many only partly overcome it," she confessed.

"Some owners are being treated for symptoms of incipient rage that certain artists they represent may not really love them. They think their artists are sending their best works to other galleries. These patients usually require long-term treatment to overcome regularly experienced sleep disorders," Dr. Kline mused.

Most Patients "Ordinary" Artists

"But most of my patients are made up of really ordinary artists like you. Some wonder if they shouldn't have taken up other hobbies. Some feel rejection from friends and family. One has given away innumerable paintings, but when she visits the homes of the giftees, the paintings are never on their walls. In another case, one of my patients found several of his paintings he had

given to some loved ones hidden under their bed.
Needless to say, he was very hurt. He is learning
to deal with their thoughtlessness and lack of taste.

I've had a number of patients who required
intensive treatment because they had taken too
many workshops and been victimized by too many
self-help books.

I've even had a 637-pound female gorilla as
a patient. I worked with her to develop a new
direction for her painting career," she said.

Dr. Kline asked me if I was often turned
down by juried shows. I told her I had my share.
When she asked if I had felt, perhaps, an
underlying anger directed at the judges who had
evidently disliked my work, I became silent.
Little tears of rage trickled down my cheeks as I
felt the bitter resentment I had been trying to stifle
all these years.

"I also conduct group sessions for artists
who are rejected from juried shows. Perhaps you
would be interested in joining one of these," she
suggested.

As I rose to leave, she handed me a typed
list of art support-groups meeting in my
neighborhood.

"I just love these gallery openings! Which gallery is this one, Gloria?

Imagine owning your own gallery with ONLY YOUR PAINTINGS hanging on the walls. Think of the prestige and the profits. No more waiting to be recognized by the art world! No humbling yourself to be represented in someone else's gallery. No more waiting for some gallery to call and tell you they sold a painting. Or worse yet, no calls from a gallery asking you to come in and pick up your work because it's not selling.

All The Sales Are Yours!
All The Money Is Yours To Keep!

No more waiting for late checks in the mail. Because when you own your own gallery, every sale and all the money is YOURS, YOURS, YOURS to keep!

Imagine the fun you'll have meeting affluent people who love your work. Watch patrons come in, pay you, and rush out of your gallery with your paintings under their arms. Think of all the fun you'll have going to the bank with envelopes full of cash and checks. Have people look up to you and be quoted by newspapers, spend hours over cocktails with RICH AND IMPORTANT PEOPLE! Listen to classical background music.

Own a gallery and be rich! Become a contributor to worthy causes, a benefactor and sponsor of other arts programs. Enjoy visits of wealthy fund-raisers who curry favor with you for donations. Get the prestigious seats at the opera and theater. Be cognizant yet seemingly unaware of the anxious and envious eyes behind those hundreds of binoculars trained upon you. They'll want to see who is that handsome and attractive gallery owner. What is she wearing? Who are those affluent, tuxedoed and richly gowned people making their way to her and engaging her in animated conversation?

Why shouldn't you have it all? Yes, you can still be a painter or sculptor and have the rich and rewarding life as a gallery owner!

Your Artist Friends Will Be GREEN With Envy!

Think of the envy your artist friends will feel when they visit your gallery and you're on the phone talking to art buyers in Chicago or Prague or London or Katmandu. Imagine how magnanimous you will be when you say, "terribly sorry" to fledgling artists who would like to be represented in your fabulous gallery where only your work will ever be shown.

See yourself gowned simply and sublimely in your latest Yves Saint Laurent with a little splash of diamonds and wearing at your wrist a tiny ruby-encrusted timepiece by Maurice Lacroix, glancing through your appointment calendar or conversing with all those eager buyers!

It's All There Waiting For You!

We have hundreds of excellent locations, new ones coming in all the time, any one JUST PERFECT for you to move into immediately. Choose from tiny 10,000 square foot starter galleries to a fourteen-story Manhattan building all your own.

All our galleries are richly furnished with deep-pile wall-to-wall carpeting and excellent track lighting. Each has a beautiful desk covered with past-due bills. Practicing with these will get you started "learning the ropes" for your new career. Each facility is left untouched just as it was on the last night when the previous owners quietly left in their vans one step ahead of the building managers.

These Are Just A Few Of The Many Letters We've Received From Ecstatic Artist-Owners:

"I could never get my paintings into juried shows. Now they beg me to be the juror!"
C. J., Elmsville, NH

"It's taken me a long time to feel this important!"
B. F., Singapore, CA

"I don't know how many galleries I tried to get my granite pieces into and was rejected by those short-sighted (expletives deleted) swine owners. Now I have ALL my pieces shown in MY gallery and I spit in their faces."
Rocky, Bainbridge Isl., WA

So don't delay. There are other painters and sculptors calling now, even as you read, to get their share of the good life as respected gallery entrepreneurs.

Just phone or fax the number on the next page. Operators are standing by day and night waiting for your call!

Volume
Galleries
CHAPTER 11

Galleries for Artists on the Go!
(and for Gallery owners also on the go!)
Call 1-800 CHA PT11
6 Bleishtiff Circle, Horvall, IL 87973.

Betsy trips her feet to Performance Art.

Chapter 17

Learn Performance Art in Your Own Home

You need not be talented

Let's say that you feel that the world is going to Perdition in a handbasket and the end of civilization as we know it is just around the corner. You want to shout or whisper that people don't care anymore, God is dead, the world is in imminent danger of complete chaos and we are on the brink of the abyss.

Let's say you are bursting with "messages" like these which you want to communicate to the world VIA ART, but you have some problems.

You can't draw, or you don't like paint, especially gooey, smelly oils, and you find waterpaints dry too fast, and you don't want to get your clothes dirty. You don't want to perform in a theater because you don't think you have any talent or can make a living at it. Yet you still want to be an artist in the worst possible way.

Try Performance Art.

Museums all over the country are clamoring for performance artists because performance artists help the directors utilize their buildings to the max. That's especially true because performance artists DON'T TAKE WALL SPACE. They only take up FLOOR SPACE and you can't *hang* paintings on the floor. Sure, most sculptures sit on the floor, but performance artists are trained to run in and out and in between pieces of sculpture without knocking things over. That's part of being a professional.

Oh. One other thing. There's no money in it. Just the thrill of being an artist and communicating! You'll have to have a job at McDonald's or marry a rich boy or girl to support you.

You're still nodding your head? Good. Now let's get started.

First you have to practice in your home without an audience. Find one or two friends who want to participate but who hate music. Give them a choice of drums, some gong-like thing, a gadget with one string which makes a sound when you hit it with a crowbar, or two sticks which are beaten against each other. BUT NOT IN RHYTHM. Make that clear.

The Message is the Medium

Now, paint your face so you are NOT YOU but the MESSAGE. Start your friends banging their instruments. Now, you run in, out, up, down. Fall down. Jump up. Take your clothes off. Have your friends take their clothes off. Sweat. Throw wadded-up newspapers. Touch each other. Grunt. Scream. Whine. Fall down together. That's it.

You can always vary the routines by wearing wigs, sheets, by being partially or wholly painted, by using tents or cardboard boxes into which you climb in and out, that kind of thing.

The message is whatever you say it is AFTER you've performed. You should have titles for your performances BEFORE the thing starts which are intentionally vague, like "Stur," or "Rampant." When audience members ask what it's all about, which they won't because they don't want to look dumb, you say it's a protest against (choose any subject which comes to your mind at the moment). It won't make any difference as long as you sound angry.

Of greatest importance is that you should not try to be entertaining. That's like selling out. The message is the thing and the more obscure, the better.

Start by performing for family and friends until you feel you're good enough to go public, hitting the museum circuit. Don't take NO for an answer from your family. Even though they may never understand what the heck you're doing, your

Mother and Dad will be proud of you. Then they will write about their "artiste" child to distant relatives, who, when they learn what you do, will be glad it costs too much to travel to see you by air or any other way.

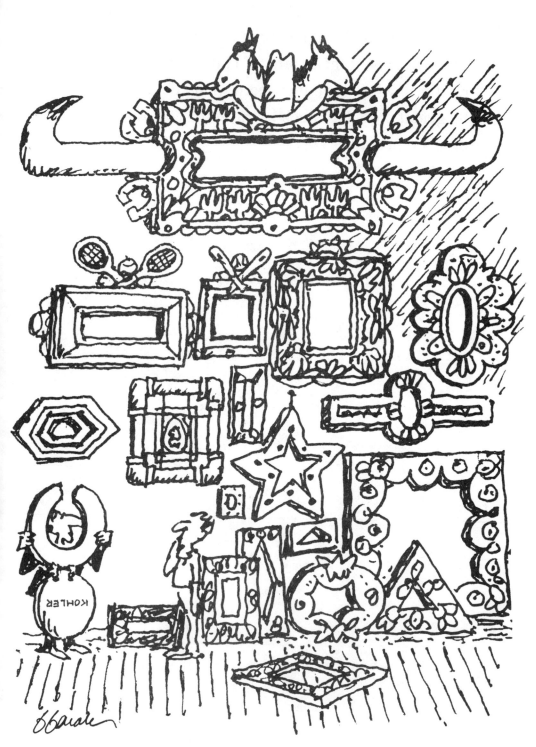

"Do you think this one is too fussy?"

Chapter 18

Create The Right Impression Through Imaginative Framing

by Studdly Snerf,* Guest Editor

*Dr. Snerf is Professor Emeritus of Framing Arts at Aschley University and author of four other books: *Precious Wood and Metal Frames I Have Loved; Framed by the FBI;* and *Going to the Mat.* In fiction, he has written: *The Sexual Frenzy of Imogene.*

Many artists never take the time or have the interest to learn about the vast array of matting and framing techniques which can turn a mediocre painting into a thing of beauty.

Say you've just painted a dog. No. Let's rephrase that. I don't want to be sued by the Association for Fairness to Canines. Let's just say that your painting lacks a certain something. That's better.

Now, if you just put that oil painting into a metal frame, maybe the painting will show up too much and possibly kill a sale or even your reputation, if you have one.

Try An Expensive Gold Frame

Your first choice should be a very expensive gold wood frame from Italy with lots of curlicues and fancy carvings. That would make it look like it belongs in a museum. Thus the viewer or potential buyer would be confused and ask himself, "Is the painting that good or is it that bad? If it's that bad, how come it's in such a beautiful frame?" See? You've introduced an element of doubt and in the process, with a little luck and the help of a good gallery salesperson, a sale just may be possible.

What would happen if you put that painting into an oval frame? Would you lose too much of the picture? Would that be bad? Try just including the best part if you can find one.

When To Use A Black Mat

A black mat can be very effective in camouflaging a mediocre watercolor. The viewer or prospect may think it somehow reveals the mood or message of your painting even though you never thought you had one when you painted it unless it resulted from a hangover or a fight with wife, kids, or the guy in the other car.

Psychological undertones in your work are good stuff. They might just make critics and jurors sit up and take notice. Who knows? A thoughtful article in an art magazine can't hurt your reputation. Especially one in which the writer attempts to describe to the public why you are using black mats. Could it be that you are attempting to express your anguish and angst over man's inhumanity to man or something deep?

Mastering The Matting Process

There are a few simple tricks to master in matting and framing your own paintings. Good tools are also vital, such as a lathe, belt sander, pneumatic drill, electric grinder, tractor, can opener, and of course, concrete nails and a sledge hammer. You may not use all these tools often but you'll be thankful they're handy when the need arises.

In addition, a good command of the language is helpful when you find you didn't measure anything right or something slipped. It's always so much more satisfying to have the right phrase on your lips when you have to throw everything away and start all over again.

Is It Worth A Mat?

Now that you have the time and the tools and you feel like framing something, take a look at your painting. Does it deserve a frame? Don't be afraid to hurt your feelings. Even if you don't, others will. But, if the answer is "YES, IT IS WORTH A FRAME," then off we go!

Start by choosing the RIGHT mat. What color mat will compliment your painting and make the best impression on the public? This is sometimes a hard choice. But to avoid a lot of indecision and head-scratching, I suggest you find out what leftover colors are being liquidated by your nearest art dealer. These colors are usually ideal and you can save yourself a lot of time by buying the cheapest. Just remember: "Hideous" is in the eye of the beholder!

Another approach is to look at your painting. If you've used lots of blue, cut a blue mat. Used lots of red? Choose a red mat. If your painting is a snow scene, glue some cotton to the mat to heighten the effect. If it's flowers, a few dead insects attached to the mat can really make the scene come alive!

Avoid Using A Chain Saw

In cutting the mat, never use a hand or chain saw because they aren't accurate unless you've had lots of practice. And your job is to paint, not be a handyman, know what I mean?

Also, when you cut the mat, be sure not to cut or scrape your fingers, because the last thing

you want on a perfectly-cut mat is blood.
Particularly yours.

Other Secrets Not Revealed

Should you use wood frames or metal?
Would I recommend your buying used metal
frames with deep scratches if the price is right?
How can you create exciting frames out of old
boxes and doors and shingles? You will want to
know the answers to questions like these if you are
going to become proficient in framing your own
paintings or take on the framing for others.

There are lots of other secrets about framing
I would like to share with you, but I won't. Heck,
who would spend the money to buy my books if I
were blabbing my head off in this article nobody's
paying me for anyway. Instead, go to your nearest
book store right now (All right, AFTER you've
eaten!) and buy a copy of my *Framing the NOW
Way.* You will find everything you ever wanted to
know right there smack dab in my book. And
don't try to return it to the book store either
because you'll probably get *shmuts* on it.

Paid Advertisements

One of the latest "In Things" to wear
to an opening.

Chapter 19

Dressing for Success!

Since earliest times, artists have

been expected to be dressed like they could afford

nice clothes. Especially those lucky enough to be born rich, have generous benefactors or who successfully painted commissioned portraits for a living.

Through the Belle Époque for example, women artists wore long dresses at the height of fashion and the men wore Edwardian suits and top hats. And it was not unusual for them even to paint in gloves.

Imagine how neat they must have been not to get *shmuts* all over their hands and clothes like we do when we paint today.

The Bohemians

During the late 1800's, the emerging artist and the public were strongly influenced by Puccini's *La Boehme*. Here young, poor, starving artists found love and joy somewhere between Starvation and Privation, two small towns on the old Luciano road to Florence.

In the opera, the players wore their best tattered and torn clothes because they were too poor to own anything else.

The production was so popular that artists started to dress and act like Bohemians just to

LOOK like artists. That meant that rich aspiring young artists had to wear rags from the Salvation Army and affect a prison pallor and a bad cough to give the impression they were dying of constipation.

Amazing Fact! Tattered suits were in such demand by wealthy upcoming or wannabe artists at that time, the Salvation Army formed a separate department to hustle up sufficient stock. They actually hired psychopaths to slash and scrape donated clothes if they weren't torn or showed hard enough use.

Threadbare Is As Dead As Fondue Pots

The pendulum has made another swing for today's artist, and threadbare is out and expensive is back in.

Take a gallery showing of one's own work. There is a very strict conservative dress code for the honoree of that affair. As many a gallery owner expects, an artist attending his opening is required to dress formally. Nylons and heels. Ties and suits. More than one gallery owner has been overheard to say to an artist, "I don't want my customers to think you're a starving artist. I want them to think they're buying the work of a successful somebody. In other words, wear a tie!"

On the opposite end of the spectrum, today's artist is expected to look -- how shall we say --- *different,* especially for gallery hopping. The more outlandish the costume, the more in, the greater the interest the general public has in attending an opening, the greater the crowd and the happier the gallery owner!

The more wildly-costumed artists are actually often sought out and often given shows of their own. A thought not lost on astute, well-dressed expectant, emerging, aspiring artists!

Barbie And I Fly To Paris

This little bit of art history is part of my all-consuming passion to know what is *in* and dress at the height of art fashion. I think an artist has an obligation to his or her public to look *right*, if you know what I mean.

So, with that thought in mind, my friend Barbie and I made our way to Paris this last Spring. There, that Mecca of haute couture design held the very first *FASHION SHOW FOR GALLERY-HOPPING ARTISTS*.

It just knocked off my Argyle socks to witness those fabulous collections on display. Here are just a few of the selections that impressed us.

For the New Woman Artist, Flashing Electrically-Lit Bras Are IN!

This year's show was all about new textiles, lacquered woods, leathers, simple shapes and NEW SURFACES.

One stunning costume by Larenta featured a slit-to-the-hip, stretch black flour sack with one gold spaghetti shoulder strap, all accessorized with a silver electrically-lit bra, used combat boots and draped around the neck, a real stuffed boa constrictor.

A standing ovation was given to a short bit of a nothing made entirely of bubble wrap and silver duct tape with matching panties. No imagination necessary on that one! Accessories included a black patent leather, silver-studded dog collar with leash, and black patent sandals with 6-

inch heels strapped over khaki camouflage anklets. Jewelry, by Slime and Grime, featured a gold lip ring and a half-carat diamond nose ring. Tattoos were by The Painful Image.

Floral Prints a Knockout

For the boys, short pants and tails in eye-shattering floral prints were a knockout. Accessories of necklaces or belts or wristlets made entirely of studded snow-chains garnered applause. Many models carried and snapped whips and blew bubble gum as they clomped down the runway in their steel-toed boots.

For the more conservative male artist, there was the loosely cut, untailored pastel suit with extra long sleeves cascading down to the knee or pushed up smartly on the arm. Pants almost completely covered their white high-topped, unlaced Nike basketball shoes. Accessories included baseball hat worn backwards, dirty undershirt, and floor-length flowered tie.

Always a great standby is the Toulouse Lautrec look-alike costume modeled by an over six foot woman. The pants are cleverly constructed so that even the tallest people, like the featured model, can walk around on their knees and look like they are short. Included are instructions for knee-walking by the actor who played "Lieutenant Dan" in the movie, *Forrest Gump*.

Well, there was much more, but for now, that's the word from Paris and you know what's IN for those important nights out or even for casual gallery hopping.

In the meantime, why not slip over to your nearest army surplus store and get some used basics for your next costume, or join the army and get it all new and free and enjoy a regular income to boot?

"Now, shall we turn on a little electricity,
Miss Shimmer, and get started?"

Chapter 20

Amazing Electronic Breakthrough!

The New Interactive Videotape Demon-stration

Thanks to the miracle of the supercomputer, the artist's videotape demonstration has reached its maturity and full potential.

From today on, aspiring painters will not simply sit in front of TV screens and watch famous artists perform demonstration paintings and wish they could duplicate them. Those days are gone, thanks to a development by Microtech, in which the amateur and famous artist are WIRED TOGETHER into the computer itself.

Demonstrator Actually A Hologram

Of course, the demonstrator is not the FAMOUS ARTIST IN PERSON, but a hologram programmed to demonstrate his technique, speak to you while you paint together, answer questions, pause at suitable times, etc. The two significant revolutionary elements which when combined make this possible, are almost beyond belief and may even signal the end of the concept of workshops.

These are the REVERSE VIDEOSENDER, a compact microrecordercamera which allows for the amazing TWO WAY HOOKUP.

Artist And Demonstrator Wired Together!

The artist and demonstrator are literally PHYSICALLY ATTACHED through wires into their computers. Each wears a wrist strap on the painting arm which has tiny wires that plug into the DEMO INLET of the computer. The hologrammed teacher can see the work of the artist as progress is made through the Reverse Videosender. This device oscillates to constantly record the student's facial expressions, lip movements, body language and the work while he paints. At the same time, the aspiring student is watching the master at work and is duplicating his painting, stroke for stroke!

When Painting Correctly, Artist Feels Almost Inexpressible Joy!

When the beginner paints an area which pleases the demonstrator, an electrical impulse is discharged into the wires attached to the beginner's wrist. Immediately, the beginner feels an almost inexpressible feeling of joy and elation.

On the other hand, when a mistake is made, a slight electrical shock is generated. This use of reward and punishment has had a remarkable success rate among test groups of rat artists.

If results do not please the student, he may restart the demonstration by simply pressing the pound button and his code to repeat the program.

The beginner is free to ask questions while the work progresses, and even to use expletives when encountering failure without offending the hologram of the instructor, which is programmed to chuckle or smile or simply ignore certain words and phrases.

There are no tapes to buy, rent or borrow. Simply type in the code and setup, and the screen shows a list of demonstrations and rates them on a scale of difficulty from 1 for rank beginner to 18 for supreme master of the medium. It is thought that many famous artists will try the 18's just to see if they can outwit other great painters.

Pollock Demo Requires 8 Cans of House Paint

Prices are also shown on the screen. Costs vary with the demonstration (two of the most expensive are Andrew Wyeth demonstrating "Ground Hog Day" and Jackson Pollock using eight cans of house paint). Not only are there substantial savings in buying or renting videotape but also in time and money spent on workshops for both the student and workshop teacher. There is nothing to pack unless one wants to pretend that a trip to a faraway warm climate is included. In that case, be sure to bring a bathing suit, shorts and a good strong sun-block in your imaginary suitcase.

There is no arriving at the workshop with jet lag and learning that you have brought all the wrong materials, no bumpy flights or layovers at the airport; no flight costs; no hotel with mattresses that are too hard, too soft or just lumpy.

There are no unfamiliar streets to get lost on. No restaurants to serve overgreasy burgers. The aspiring artist can turn the system off at any time and run to the refrigerator as often as he or she likes for a reward or maybe for just a little emotional comfort.

And most important for the student, he doesn't have to look at and envy the work of other artists in a class with resultant depression and loss of confidence.

For more information on this new development, connect your computer with Internet and key in "Demonstrations, Artist, Interactive.com."

Can Your Cat Draw This Cat?

**How many famous cats began their
careers in art.**

You and your cat have probably seen our ads on the bags and cans of your favorite pet food. Perhaps you've both entertained the idea of enrollment in the Cyrus Academy of Realist Cat Art By And For Cats, but have hesitated. Could it be that your cat wanted more information or you felt he, she or it wasn't ready or maybe not sufficiently artistically inclined?

Allow me to take this opportunity to tell you about The School and its high standards and to answer some of your unanswered questions.

"Why Cats Paint"*
Deeply Concerns Cyrus

Cyrus Academy, etc., was established four years ago, I'm proud to say, by our resident Himalayan cat, Cyrus. The Academy and its course of study were the result of ideas which matured in his mind over seven years of almost continuous napping. Recently, he had come across the book, "Why Cats Paint,"* by Heather Busch and Burton Silver. It describes and illustrates how a number of cats paint in various abstract styles.

Cyrus came to live with us after he was trained in classical art by the famous Persian realist cat, Mahmoud Ben Amahl (1967-1987). Cyrus was known throughout the world for his realist or impressionistic style. His paintings are included in the Friskie Collection and he was the author of "Cat Painting for Cats" (Simon Press, 1989).

Book Convinces Cyrus To Expand School Immediately!

Until he scanned the "Why Cats Paint" book (he did admire the photographs), the Academy was a purely local venture and he enrolled mainly neighborhood cats. However, the book changed his attitude markedly and he decided to reach out nationally for cat art students via advertisements mentioned earlier. Cyrus felt that "Why Cats Paint" is suggesting that all a cat has to do is get some paint on his, her or its paws to become painter.

"Nothing can be further from the truth," he growled. "Being an artist cat takes training and dedication, just like any other occupation for cats. There is no easy road to success. Besides," he confided, "when I see a painting of a cat or a bird, or a mouse, I want it to look like the real thing! Not just a bunch of claw and paw marks."

Today, the school remains true to the ideals and concepts of Cyrus, its architect and founder, and is known throughout the world of cat art as the leading school in its field.

Students who meet the criteria will reside at The Academy, located in beautiful, cat-friendly Lake Oswego, Oregon. The campus stretches over a quarter of a block of lovely rolling grass and tall fir trees with a view of the lake. All cat students are welcome to spray favorite areas to feel really at home while enrolled at the Academy.

There are no sororities or fraternities on campus. Cyrus Academy is an equal opportunity institution. All felines are accorded the same considerate treatment regardless of breed, sex or lack of it, or family wealth. However, in the interest of maintaining the highest academic standards, Cyrus insists that each applicant come to the school with serious intentions.

Healthy, nutritious meals are provided, though pet owners may send treats occasionally for their loved ones.

Little personal touches include two spacious compartmentalized litter boxes both indoors and out for privacy and comfort. Sleeping quarters are arranged so that each student has a down-filled pillow in his, her or its own basket.

No Kittens Accepted, Please

Classes are limited to six students per 3-week term. Cats must be mature and prepared to work hard for the 45 minutes of class periods before they curl up for their 18 hours of sleep.

They must be healthy and really serious about art. Cyrus Academy does not accept kittens. The administration does not feel they make suitable candidates, no matter how talented, because they lack concentration and spend too much time looking cute and playing with yarn.

Through the course, applicants gain a strong foundation in feline anatomy by drawing and painting from the nude cat. Other classes include color theory, basic design, painting on paper, wallpaper, cardboard and textiles. The final session is devoted to teaching applicants how to get gallery representation.

Graduation is particularly impressive with a ceremony in which graduates get their diplomas in full regalia of little caps and gowns. Following matriculation, the Academy attempts to place many of its graduate cats in high-paying art careers.

Ask About Cyrus' "Lend a Paw" Scholarships

Fees are based on a sliding scale, but no deserving cat is ever turned away. The Academy's famous "Lend a Paw" scholarship program is always ready to help. Here cats earn their tuition by hunting and ridding the campus of moths, flies, rodents and other pesky game.

There are rules, of course, which students must respect while on campus. Scratching of furniture or hopping on beds, chairs or sofas with painty paws is cause for suspension. Candidates must confine themselves to the school's sandboxes and not use Cyrus' private litterbox. Use of catnip is strictly limited as is night life.

Learn More Today!

If you or your cat feel that he, she or it has the necessary qualifications and would like to make a career in art, write for a prospectus:

CYRUS ACADEMY OF REALIST CAT ART

Box C.A.T., Lake Oswego OR 97034

THE school for the career-minded artistic cat

Please do not call.
Cyrus does not have opposable thumbs and
cannot answer the phone.

Letters to the Editor:

Accuses Unfair Treatment

I am a mature, worldly-wise Alaskan Husky dog who generally reads and chews on your publication, ads and all with great relish. But this time you've gone too far. Your ad for the Cyrus Academy of Realist Cat Art by and for Cats offends my intelligence and nobility.

Who are you to suggest that only cats have deep emotional needs that must be met by artistic endeavor? I have been painting for the past five years -- off and on between runs, of course -- and I've been told that my works display a strong urgency not unlike those of the famous 19th Century Chow, Wa Chang. So how about some equal opportunity ads from now on? We canines may have to work for a living, but we have our sensitive sides, too.

Editor's Reply:

We regret we may have suggested in any way that our publication caters only to cats, gorillas and humanoids. We value our canine subscribers and will endeavor in future to include articles of particular interest to them. We are at this very moment, contacting art schools which train dogs for careers in art and will include that listing once we find such an institution.

If you wish to express your viewpoint to this publication, write:
The Editor, Letterbox L, Stanhope MU 66094

If you are a fur-covered, four legged creature, please have a two-legged creature type your letters double-spaced. We are having trouble reading your paw scratches otherwise.

--the Editor

Heed the word! GET TO WORK!

The Inspirational Hour

Try Five Of My Twelve Steps To Increased Creative Motivation!

I don't know how many people have asked me, "Where do you find the inspiration to pursue your art?" Wow! Now, isn't that the most fundamental question about the whole darn art-thing!

Inspiration is so absolutely central and essential to my creative process that I thought I would share some really deep feelings and suggestions with you.

Inspiration doesn't come easy. It requires a consistent regimen, both physical and mental. First, we are physical beings. Our minds are attached to our bodies with bone, sinew and muscle. Those wonderful bodies need exercise and nurturing in order to provide a strong yet loving home for our brains so they can do their best work! When they are in a good home, they are happy blobs of gray cells and really excited to serve their thinker. Doesn't that make darn good sense? That's why I start with my 13-point physical list:

My One-Hour Physical Regimen

Step 1: Physical Conditioning

I have developed a program which I have taped to a wall near my easel. My list of exercises has been collected from a variety of health publications I have read while waiting in doctor and dentist offices. The regimen I recommend starts with 10 minutes of stretching, followed by 20 minutes of vigorous movements which sends the heart rate up to 1 million units per second. Within 20 minutes, one should complete:

- 10 sit ups
- 25 push ups
- 25 pull ups
- 18 spiral twists to left
- 18 spiral twists to right
- 22 yoga locks, snake position
- 19 unwinders
- 25 deep knee bends with 50 pound weights
- 3 minutes, head stand
- 15 one-handed hand stands
- 15 handstands on one finger
- 30 seconds rest
- run fourteen miles

Did You Get That All Copied Down? Good.

I look at this list, read it carefully and am completely inspired to sit down immediately and start painting. It takes little more than knowing I don't have to do it that really gets me going in the morning. You should find it equally efficacious in your inspirational program as well.

Now, let's say that doesn't work. If after reading my PHYSICAL REGIMEN over two or three times, inspiration doesn't come, then please follow me as I go to Step 2.

Step 2: Go To Refrigerator

I don't know why it works so well, but just the minute I open the refrigerator door and see the little light go on behind the chilling wine bottles, a little bell inside my head goes ding dong! I simply feel charged, inspirationally, that is. And I feel like going back to paint as soon as I've looked inside and gathered up some really thought-provoking treats.

If you choose this approach to inspiration, I urge you to exercise some caution. Do not use anything which has to be heated, because by the time it's warm, some of your inspiration may have evaporated. Or worse yet, you may have forgotten why you went to the refrigerator in the first place. Secondly, do not eat everything on those lovely shelves. Leave a few morsels for the time you may need more inspiration -- say ten minutes from now.

Bear in mind, that all my inspirational tools require some patience and take some practice. But let's say the first two aren't working for you. Then try Step 3:

Step 3: Walk To The Store

If your nearest store is less than four blocks away, get some exercise by walking. If it's further than that, drive and find little goodies that will satisfy your inspirational needs. Eat the Snickers and the Hershey bar on the way home so you won't get chocolate fingerprints on your work. Put the rest in the fridge for a later dose.

Didn't work? Hmmm. All right. It's time for Step 4.

Step 4: Go Back To Sleep

Maybe your inspiration is still in bed. Heh, heh, heh. But what if all you need is sleep. You must return to the bedroom, hop in bed and take it. I can't emphasize this strongly enough! Your body and your brain are telling you sleep is THAT IMPORTANT and you must listen to your inner ticking clock!

Take at least one more hour to get a good nap or take whatever time your body needs for rest. And when you rise and get dressed, you will find you have a full load of inspiration. Then, take up your palette and paint brush or wet clay or whatever medium you're using, and you'll find you will do wonderful things.

But say this particular time, nothing seems to be working. Don't look so frustrated. It only means you're ready for Step 5:

Step 5: Talk To Father Ribaldo At St. Anthony's

Go to St. Anthony's on SW Alder and visit with the good father. Listen carefully to his inspirational message:

"INDOLENCE IS SINFUL! NEVER MIND SITTING ON YOUR BOTTOM AND TALKING INSPIRATIONAL NONSENSE! YOU WANT TO PAINT? PAINT! GOD HELPS THOSE WHO HELP THEMSELVES! GO TO WORK, MY SON (DAUGHTER)!

If you are interested in my

"12 STEPS TO HIGHER AWARENESS,"

send a stamped, self-addressed envelope to:

The Inspirational Hour

Box Q, Lincoln, WA 00068
Or call 900-ANY-HOUR

Press 1 if you need immediate guidance. **Press 4** for complete menu. Press **5** if you think you have the wrong number. Press **7** if you would like to hear all this repeated. Press **all the keys at once** if you feel frustration.
If you get a busy signal, you will know that someone else is receiving inspiration. But please stay on the line because your call is important to us.

Paid Advertisements

Author's Note

Frank Sullivan was a wonderful humorist and contributor to the New Yorker some years ago. He wrote among his many books, a hilarious one entitled as I recall, , "In The Worst Possible Taste."

I humbly entertain the hope that this book contributes in some small way to that lofty ideal.

---*Arne Westerman*

Glossary

Abstract Expressionism. Emotionally driven non-representational paintings, usually grotesque and ugly. Better buy something you like.

Angst. How about looking up something yourself? Oh, all right. It means feeling of dread.

Bright. A flat, thin, oil painting brush with a straight sharp end, invented by an English artist. Guess his name.

Brussels Sprouts and Liver with Onions. Two inedible foods first cultivated by sadistic savages. Eat only if you need to add to your misery.

Driblick. Six and seven-thirty-sevenths to the Guilder in 1638.

Esperanto. I think it's like Spanish.

Exercycle. A bicycle type exercise machine always found at garage sales, sometimes in the company of stair-steppers and other athletic equipment.

Gioconda. The family name of the sitter who posed for the painting of the Mona Lisa, we think.

Gornisht. Nothing. Nothing at all.

Hedonistic Impracticism. Anything the artist likes but can't sell. See "impractical".

Hog Bristle Filbert. A flat oil-paint brush shaped like an oval, made of the hair of pigs not fast enough to get away.

Kinetic Abstraction. Non-representational paintings usually executed by gymnastic painters.
Meshuge. (Page 58) Mad, insane, crazy, nuts.

Meshuge. Mad, insane, crazy, nuts.

Mikvah or Mikve. A ritual bath used for purification.

Muffie. Girls are named Muffie in honor of this first independent, Neanderthal woman vegetarian.

Nebish. An unfortunate.

Neo-Geo-Ablutionism. Abstract painting or sculpture dunked in a Mikvah for ritual purification and improvement. Not advised for reviving a watercolor. See "Mikvah."

Neo-Geo-Sumo-Wrestlingism. Abstract installation using flour sacks with violence. A favorite artistic expression of ex-wrestlers.

Palette Knife, No. 7. Between a No. 6 and a No. 8.

Primevalism. Unabashed copies of cave painting techniques.

Quotidian. Daily, ordinary, everyday. Burt Silverman uses big words.

Realisiticism. A work of art so real it can actually be used for the real thing such as a car which can be driven,

Schnorer. A beggar.

Shmuts. Dirt or garbage.

Shrying. Crying or wailing.

Tire Kickers. People who look at but don't buy paintings. *Origin: Used-car dealers.*

Tsores. Troubles.

About Arne Westerman

Arne Westerman is a painter, teacher and writer in that order. He is a member of the American Watercolor Society, the National Watercolor Society the Northwest and Oregon societies. He has won a number of grand prizes in juried exhibitions and teaches art workshops throughout the United States. His work is included in museums and other public and private collections. His paintings are featured in several galleries including Zantman Galleries, Carmel, California and at the Attic Gallery in Portland, Oregon. He is represented in Washington DC by the Galerie DeTours. Arne works out of his studio in Portland, Oregon.